Enjoy the songs!
Robert Gogan

50 Great Irish Fighting Songs

ROBERT GOGAN

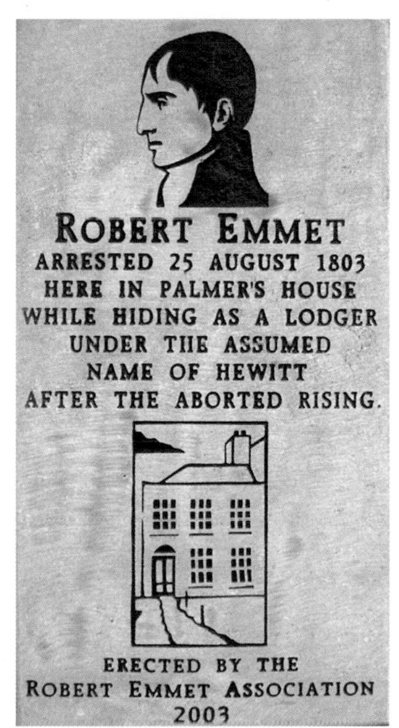

Music Ireland

Published by Music Ireland, 61 Grosvenor Square, Rathmines, Dublin 6, Ireland.

Printed by: Everbest Printing Company, Hong Kong
Designed by: Robert Gogan
Cover/CD design by: MGA Design Consultants, Dublin
Photographs: Robert Gogan, Anne Tyrrell.
Front cover: 1798 memorial, Dunlavin, Wicklow.
Back cover: 1798 Memorial, Glenmalure, Wicklow.
Photo previous page: At Palmer's House, Dublin.

Accompanying CD recorded at Sonic Studios, Dublin.
Engineer: Al Cowan
Producer: Robert Gogan
Musicians
Vocals: Sinéad Martin. John Doyle. Robert Gogan. Anne Tyrrell
Guitar: Sinéad Martin. Roddy Gallagher. Robert Gogan.

ISBN 0 9532068 7 4

Bunratty Castle, Clare.
This mainly 15th century castle played an important part in the struggles between the Anglo-Norman de Clares and the Thomond forces in the 13th century

POBLACHT NA H EIREANN.

THE PROVISIONAL GOVERNMENT

OF THE

IRISH REPUBLIC

TO THE PEOPLE OF IRELAND.

IRISHMEN AND IRISHWOMEN: In the name of God and of the dead generations from which she receives her old tradition of nationhood, Ireland, through us, summons her children to her flag and strikes for her freedom.

Having organised and trained her manhood through her secret revolutionary organisation, the Irish Republican Brotherhood, and through her open military organisations, the Irish Volunteers and the Irish Citizen Army, having patiently perfected her discipline, having resolutely waited for the right moment to reveal itself, she now seizes that moment, and, supported by her exiled children in America and by gallant allies in Europe, but relying in the first on her own strength, she strikes in full confidence of victory.

We declare the right of the people of Ireland to the ownership of Ireland, and to the unfettered control of Irish destinies, to be sovereign and indefeasible. The long usurpation of that right by a foreign people and government has not extinguished the right, nor can it ever be extinguished except by the destruction of the Irish people. In every generation the Irish people have asserted their right to national freedom and sovereignty; six times during the past three hundred years they have asserted it in arms. Standing on that fundamental right and again asserting it in arms in the face of the world, we hereby proclaim the Irish Republic as a Sovereign Independent State, and we pledge our lives and the lives of our comrades-in-arms to the cause of its freedom of its welfare, and of its exaltation among the nations.

The Irish Republic is entitled to, and hereby claims, the allegiance of every Irishman and Irishwoman. The Republic guarantees religious and civil liberty, equal rights and equal opportunities to all its citizens, and declares its resolve to pursue the happiness and prosperity of the whole nation and of all its parts, cherishing all the children of the nation equally, and oblivious of the differences carefully fostered by an alien government, which have divided a minority from the majority in the past.

Until our arms have brought the opportune moment for the establishment of a permanent National Government, representative of the whole people of Ireland and elected by the suffrages of all her men and women, the Provisional Government, hereby constituted, will administer the civil and military affairs of the Republic in trust for the people.

We place the cause of the Irish Republic under the protection of the Most High God. Whose blessing we invoke upon our arms, and we pray that no one who serves that cause will dishonour it by cowardice, inhumanity, or rapine. In this supreme hour the Irish nation must, by its valour and discipline and by the readiness of its children to sacrifice themselves for the common good, prove itself worthy of the august destiny to which it is called.

Signed on Behalf of the Provisional Government,

THOMAS J. CLARKE.

SEAN Mac DIARMADA. THOMAS MacDONAGH,

P. H. PEARSE, EAMONN CEANNT,

JAMES CONNOLLY. JOSEPH PLUNKETT

The Proclamation of the Republic of Ireland, read out by Padraig Pearse from the steps of the General Post Office, O'Connell Street, Dublin, on the first day of the 1916 Rebellion

Introduction

"The Fighting Irish" is a phrase well-known throughout the world and there's good reason for this! Whether on the sports field, in a dancehall or at a wake, the Irish have always shown a willingness to enter into a bout of fisty-cuffs at the drop of a hat. Who can forget the memorable fight scene in "The Quiet Man" when the whole town came out to witness and enjoy the spectacle of a 'harmless Donnybrook'! Yes, you could say that the Irishman has always stood his ground and fought his corner!

A more serious fight - the struggle for an independent nation - pre-occupied many brave Irish people over a span of hundreds of years. Countless fine ballads were composed to lay witness to the events, praise the heroes and lament the defeats. And defeats there were plenty! But the Irish came back fighting again and again and again and, in the face of far greater odds, eventually forged a nation of which we can all rightly be proud.

Many of those individuals who made the ultimate sacrifice for their ideals are remembered in ballads in this book. Let's sing them with pride and never forget that the sacrifices made by these patriots were made by them for the future generations. And we are that future generation.

I am indebted to the following publications and websites for facts, information and references and for pointing me in the right direction:

"The Petrie Collection of Ancient Music of Ireland" edited by David Cooper. Cork University Press
"The Irish Music Manuscripts of Edward Bunting (1773 - 1843). An Introduction and Catalogue" edited by Colette Moloney. Irish Traditional Music Archive.
"Folksongs of Britain and Ireland" edited by Peter Kennedy. Cassell
"The Complete Guide to Celtic Music" by June Skinner Sawyers. Aurum Press
"The Age of Revolution in the Irish Song Tradition 1776 - 1815" edited by Terry Moylan. Lilliput Press
"Songs of Irish Rebellion" by Georges-Denis Zimmerman. Allen Figgis
"Irish Ballads" edited by Fleur Robertson. Gill & MacMillan
"The Poolbeg Book of Irish Ballads" by Sean McMahon. Poolbeg Press
"The '98 Reader" edited by Padraic O'Farrell. Lilliput Press
"The Oxford Companion to Irish History" edited by S.J. Connolly. Oxford University Press
"The Year of Liberty" by Thomas Pakenham. Abacus
"The Easter Rebellion" by Max Caulfield. Gill & MacMillan
"AA Illustrated Road Book of Ireland" Automobile Association
"The Encyclopaedia of Ireland" edited by Brian Lalor. Gill & McMillan
www.contemplator.com/folk
www.mudcat.org
www.standingstones.com
www.kued.org/joehill

The CD

If you are not familiar with the particular melody of a song and can't read music the accompanying CD will provide you with the basic tune.

The Chorus

If a song has a chorus it is printed in bold italics ***like this***. Some songs start with a chorus and therefore it will be in the main body of the score. Others have the chorus after the first verse. Choruses are great things - they are a law unto themselves. You can add more in (and this normally depends on the number of verses of the ballad you know!) or take them out if you want to shorten the song.

So do your own thing! Do it your way!

But above all, enjoy these songs! They are crying out to be sung!

Robert Gogan

Index By Song Title

Index By CD Track

Index By First Line

Guitar Chords used in this book

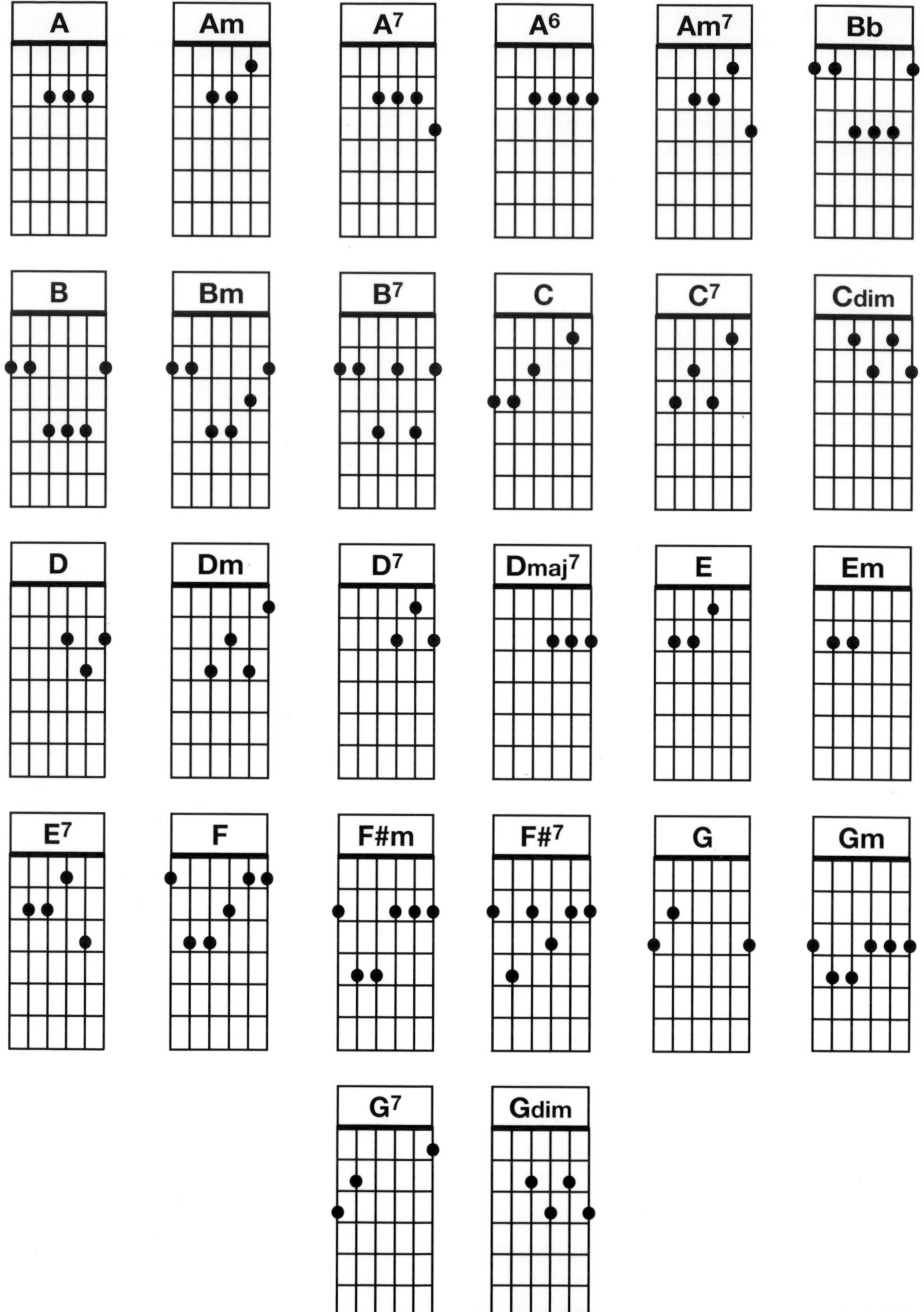

Dwyer - McAllister Cottage, Doirenamuc, Wicklow
Fleeing after the 1798 Rebellion, Michael Dwyer, Samuel McAllister and others took refuge in this cottage on the snowey night of 15th February 1799. Their hide-out was betrayed to the English who immediately beseiged it. When McAllister was wounded in the arm he realised that he could not avoid capture. He went to the front door and voluntary drew all gunfire upon himself, thus sufficiently distracting attention to allow Dwyer to escape unharmed. Dwyer later emigrated to Australia where he died in 1829. The cottage has been partially reconstructed and contains furnishings of a type used around 1798.

Additional Notes

1798 Insurrection

The rebellion of 1798 took place throughout many regions of Ireland between May 23rd (when fighting started in Dublin, Kildare and Meath) and September 23rd (the collapse of the Mayo rising).
The rebellion was planned and led by the Society of United Irishmen, comprised mainly of the Irish middle classes. This society was established in Belfast on October 18th, 1791, and in Dublin on November 9th.
The United Irishmen spanned religious boundaries. The majority of the members of the Belfast section was Presbyterian and the Dublin section was divided equally between Catholics and Protestants.
Inspired by the recent American and French Revolutions the objectives of the United Irishmen were to purge English influence in Ireland and to reform the parliament so that English control over Irish affairs would be terminated.
The English authorities sought to destroy the United Irishmen. In May 1794 the Dublin society was suppressed, provoking the Belfast society to re-organise itself into a secret oath-bound society, planning for armed insurrection.
The 1798 Rebellion was more widespread throughout Ireland than other rebellions, with action taking place in :-
1. Dublin, Kildare and Meath on the east coast. English forces killed over 300 insurgents at Tara, County Meath, and 200 at the Curragh in Kildare. The insurgents then attempted to capture Carlow town but were heavily defeated on May 26th.
2. Eastern Ulster, including Antrim. The United Irishmen had a strong organisation in Ulster. Their main campaigns in the 1798 Rebellion centred around the towns of Antrim and Ballynahinch. The Ulster United Irishmen received less support than they had anticipated from the Antrim Catholics and due to some poor organisation and morale, and treachery, the Government forces soon regained control.
3. County Wexford, where some of the fiercest fighting took place. The uprising began there on May 26th. The town of Enniscorthy was captured on May 28th and Wexford town on May 30th. However on June 5th the insurgents lost over 2,000 men at the Battle of New Ross. At the Battle of Arklow on June 9th about 350 insurgents were killed. On June 21st the English forces stormed Vinegar Hill outside Enniscorthy and defeated the 20,000 strong insurgent force. Wexford town was also recaptured on that day thereby quenching the Wexford chapter of the rebellion.
4. Connaught, sparked off by the landing of the French expedition at Killala Bay, County Mayo, under General Humbert on August 22nd. General Humbert was forced to surrender to the English on September 8th and the Connaught rising ended with the recapture of Killala on September 23rd.
The 1798 Rebellion is regarded as the most brutal and tragic event in Irish history. Over 30,000 Irish men and women were killed, murdered or executed in a period of eighteen weeks by the better equipped and trained English forces.
If you are ever in the town of Enniscorthy you should visit 'Aras 1798' - the '1798 Centre'. Through audio visual presentations and displays you will experience a very comprehensive overview of the rebellion. The Centre traces the 1798 Rebellion in Ireland through the use of multi-media technology, culminating in a 3D simulation of the Battle of Vinegar Hill, one of the most important battles in the rebellion.
There are seven ballads in this book relating to the 1798 Rebellion:-
"Boulavogue" (page 68) celebrates the exploits of Father John Murphy, one of the leaders of the Wexford rebellion.
"The Croppy Boy" (page 70) narrates the treachery of the loyalists during the rebellion.
"Kelly From Killane" (page 60) commemorates John Kelly, one of the leaders of the attack on New Ross.
"The Rising Of The Moon" (page 20) recounts the rebellion in County Longford.
"Roddy McCorley" (page 77) laments the execution of Roddy McCorley, who took part in the rebellion in Antrim.
"The Boys of Wexford" (page 28) sings the praises of the Wexford insurgents.
"Dunlavin Green" (page 48) mourns the massacre of thirty-six men in that village.

Rebellion of 1803 - Emmet's Rebellion

This failed attempt to unseat British power in Ireland was the last throw of the dice for the United Irishmen, whose recent Insurrection of 1798 had ended in defeat and nationwide bloodshed.
As with many other rebellions the leaders were relying on support from abroad - this time from France - but it didn't materialise.
The organisers of the rebellion were mainly veterans of 1798 - Thomas Russell, Myles Byrne and Michael Quigley. A young romantic nationalist, Robert Emmet was chosen to be the leader of the Dublin corridore of the rebellion. As action only took place in Dublin it rapidly became known as Emmet's Rebellion.
Emmet was a student of Trinity College, Dublin. He was expelled from the college for his nationalist opinions in April 1798.
In 1800 he travelled to France to solicit assistance for another rebellion but was unsuccessful. He returned to Ireland in October 1802.

By early 1803 Emmet was fully occupied in organising an uprising against the British occupiers. Weapons were stockpiled and supporters recruited.

Following an explosion at the arms depot in Patrick Street on July 16th 1803, Emmet decided to bring the rebellion forward to July 23rd. Though not yet fully prepared his hope was that, following the seizure of strategic buildings in Dublin, there would be a spontaneous popular uprising throughout the country.

On July 23rd only a small number of the expected insurgents assembled. The attack on Dublin Castle, the seat of British rule in Ireland, was abandoned and the band of insurgents soon degenerated into an unruly mob. About 50 people were killed in the ensuing rioting, including Lord Kilwarden, the former Attorney-General, and Arthur Wolfe, Lord Chief Justice.

Emmet fled to a house in Harold's Cross, then a village to the south of the city, masquerading as a lodger under the name of Hewitt. He was arrested on August 25th and executed on September 20th in front of St. Catherine's Church, Thomas Street.

Emmet quickly became a romantic icon in Irish history. Successive nationalist and revoloutionary movements regarded him as the young heroic idealistic revolutionary to which their sympathisers and supporters should aspire.

During his trial, his speech from the dock is considered to be one of the finest courtroom orations in Irish history and was memorised by many's a nationalist and recited frequently at social and political gatherings.

The reality that his rebellion was little more than an urban skirmish has been conveniently overlooked. In the hearts of Irish people he was regarded with admiration for his idealistic, if somewhat youthful expectations, and his willingness to make the ultimate sacrifice.

There are many ballads dedicated to the memory of Robert Emmet. Undoubtedly the most popular is "Bold Robert Emmet" (page 75)

Young Ireland and 'The Nation' - 1848

The Young Ireland Movement was established informally in 1842 by a group of nationalists, keen to disassociate themselves from the O'Connell Repeal movement.

Following on the Paris Revolution of 1848 the leaders of Young Ireland decided to strike for independence. They were romantic idealists, unprepared for the harsh realities of revolution. The movement was comprehensively infiltrated by spies and informers who kept the British authorites fully informed of developments.

They lacked a coherent plan of action and incorrectly assumed, like so many previous revolutionaries, that a sporadic popular uprising would occur as soon as word spread that an official rebellion had started.

Following on an inoffensive encounter with British forces in Tipperary on July 28th 1848 there followed a skermish at Ballingarry, Tipperary in the widow McCormick's farmhouse, in which two insurgents were killed. The crowd of about 100 poorly armed peasants dispersed. Some of the leaders escaped to America; others were convicted of treason and transported to Australia in 1849.

'The Nation' was a weekly newspaper founded in 1842 and its aim was the promotion of cultural nationalism. It was the voice of the Young Ireland movement.

Its promoters were Thomas Davis, John Blake Dillon and Charles Gavan Duffy, all Young Ireland leaders.

'The Nation', as with the Young Ireland movement itself, sought to evoke a sense of national pride through literature and song and preached the revival of ancient Gaelic traditions. Its founders were aware of the capacity of song to instil a sense of nationality into the common people. "We furnish political songs" it was quoted in one of the issues, "to stimulate flagging zeal, or create it where it does not exist".

The type of nationalist ballad promoted by 'The Nation' was primarily of a literary nature as opposed to the blood-thirsty broadside ballads composed as a spontaneous reaction to political events.

'The Nation' invited and encouraged poets and balladeers from the four corners of Ireland to submit suitable works for publication. Thomas Davis in particular was aware of the power of the political ballad as propaganda.

'The Nation' set about systematically publishing songs, ballads and poems based on incidents in Irish history and the nationalist aspirations of its people. It became immensely popular. With an initial print-run of 12,000 the newspaper claimed to have a readership of about 250,000, the paper being handed around from home to home and parish to parish until it literally fell apart.

Davis himself wrote about 50 ballads which were published in 'The Nation'. Two of his works are included in this book: "The West's Awake" (page 74) and "A Nation Once Again" (page 62). Many other ballads in this book were first presented to the Irish public through the pages of 'The Nation'.

The best of the ballads printed in the first six months of 'The Nation' were published in a book in May 1843 under the title "The Spirit of the Nation, by Writers of The Nation Newspaper". A second book was published in November 1843. Both titles were phenomenal successes.

In 1848 'The Nation' was suppressed by the British authorities because of its revolutionary tendencies.

Gavan Duffy was allowed to relaunch it in 1849 but it never attained the heights of its former glory.
It merged temporarily with 'The Irish Catholic' from 1891 to 1896 and ceased publication in 1900, merging with the 'Irish Weekly Independent'.

The Fenian Rising of 1867

The Fenian movement was established as a successor to the Young Ireland movement of the 1840's. The principle protagonists, and initial supporters, emanated from the Irish immigrant communities in the USA. Men like John O'Mahony, Michael Doheny and James Stephens were determined to establish the Fenians as a revolutionary society, dedicated to secrecy and to the overthrow of British occupation in Ireland.
The movement was launched in Dublin on St. Patrick's Day 1858.
As so many previous uprising attempts in Ireland had been thwarted by informers and drunken loud-mouths, Stephens set up a hierarchical structure whereby each member of the movement would only have information about the immediate comrades in his own section.
Unfortunately the general organisation, and the common practice within the movement, paid little heed to Stephens' expectations.
As the movement spread nationwide it attracted the unwanted attention of the British authorities, who quickly and easily infiltrated the organisation. In 1865 they swooped and arrested the leaders in Ireland and suppressed the movement's newspaper, "The Irish People".
Informers and leadership splits undermined the effectiveness and determination of the movement to stage an uprising. A weak attempt was made in February 1867, followed by a more determined effort on the night of 4-5 March 1867 but neither amounted to anything.
The main significance of the Fenian movement was in its legacy and aspirations. The movement kept the flame of revolution alive among nationalists, so severely weakened after the 1798 Insurrection. It fostered the realisation that, some day, there would be a popular uprising against British rule in Ireland which would be successful and lead to the establishment of an independent Irish State.
Nationalist opinion was mobilised following the execution of the Manchester Martyrs (see page 8), and renewed demands for an amnesty for Fenian prisoners. This lead to the formation of a new movement, the Irish Republican Brotherhood, with a determined philosophy that armed revolt was the only way to gain independence The IRB set the stage for the 1916 Rebellion, the War of Independence and eventually for Irish Sovereignty.
The label 'Fenian' became synonymous with 'rebel' and is used to this present day by loyalists.
There are references to Fenians in many songs in this book, in particular
"Bold Fenian Men" (page 10)
"God Save Ireland" (page 8)

Easter Rising 1916

The Easter Rising was fought over six days during Easter Week 1916.
There were three main Nationalist organisations operating in Ireland at that time: (a) The Irish Volunteers formed in 1913, a movement originally established to act as a defence against the Ulster Volunteers. Its Commander-in-Chief in 1916 was Eoin McNeill, (b) The Irish Republican Brotherhood, a revolutionary organisation which evolved out of the Fenian movement of the 1860's. Many of the Easter Rising leaders came from its inner council including Thomas Clarke and Sean McDermott, and (c) The Irish Citizen Army established by The Irish Transport and General Workers Union to protect striking workers and pickets during the notorious Dublin lockout of 1913. James Connolly was its Commandant.
The 1916 Rising was planned by a Military Council established in 1915 by the Supreme Council of the Irish Republican Brotherhood. They collaborated with Padraig Pearse, Joseph Plunkett, Thomas McDonagh and Eamon Ceannt, all prominent members of the Volunteers. In January 1916 James Connolly was initiated into the conspiracy.
The planners feared that Eoin McNeill might not endorse the rising so they withheld the plans from him.
The leaders envisaged a general rising throughout the entire country and it certainly appeared that they had the manpower within the three organisations to realise this ambition.
However they didn't have the ammunition and weapons to achieve their goal. The leaders looked to Germany for assistance and the German Admiralty agreed to provide a supply of weapons and ammunition for the rising.
However, the arrangements to land the arms failed miserably.
By this time Eoin McNeill had learned of the plans and had reluctantly agreed to support the rising. However, when he heard of the failure to land the arms and realised that the insurgents were almost completely without weapons and ammunition he published an order in the Sunday Independent cancelling all Volunteer 'manoeuvres' scheduled for Sunday April 23rd. Most of the Volunteers obeyed this order and consequently the leaders of the rising could only muster a small

portion of the potential force and it was decided to strike on Easter Monday.
The rising began on Easter Monday, April 24th, when about 1,000 Irish Volunteers and 200 members of the Irish Citizen Army seized the General Post Office and other strategic sites in Dublin. Fighting continued until the insurgents surrendered on April 29th.
The official death toll was 64 insurgents, 132 British soldiers and about 230 civilians. Extensive use of heavy artillery by the British laid waste large areas of the city centre. There were supported actions in Wexford, Galway and County Dublin and an attempted mobilisation in Cork.
The Easter Rising was a fairly unique rebellion insofar as the leaders, when they learned of the fate of the German arms, fully accepted that there was absolutely no prospect of success. However they decided to proceed in the hope that their action would awaken nationalist pride and revolutionary spirit among the Irish people.
There was widespread and open hostility among the Dublin population towards the insurgents during and immediately after the rising. This sentiment changed to sympathy and then outright support as the British administration adopted a hard line approach and executed fifteen of the leaders along with Sir Roger Casement, who had convinced the Germans to supply weapons.
There are three ballads in this book relating to the Easter Rising:-
"Banna Strand" (page 66) laments the failure to land the German arms and ammunition in Kerry.
"The Foggy Dew" (page 26) applauds the bravery of the insurgents who mobilised and fought in the rising.
"James Connolly" (page 2) mourns the execution of the commandant of The Irish Citizen Army.

The Black and Tans

In the immediate aftermath of the 1916 Rebellion, the various militant nationalist organisations formed themselves into the Irish Republican Army (IRA) and they conducted frequent effective guerilla attacks against the British institutions in Ireland, with considerable success.
The regular police force, the Royal Irish Constabulary, was rapidly becoming ineffective against the IRA and the British Government decided that it needed swift reinforcement. Recruitment began in January 1920. By November 1921 about 9,500 men, mainly British ex-soldiers and sailors, had joined the RIC.
There was a shortage of RIC uniforms and the new recruits were issued with khaki military trousers and dark green police tunics. Thus the nickname 'Black and Tans' came into being.
The Black and Tans were poorly trained and lacked discipline. The IRA took them on head-to-head.
A second independent group, recruited from among de-militarised British Army officers and officially known as the Auxiliary Division of the RIC was also labelled with the nickname 'Black and Tans'. This group consisted of about 1,900 men and in practice operated independently of the RIC. They were heavily armed and highly mobile. Their mandate, though never acknowledged by the British authorities, was to vigorously pursue the IRA and to use whatever means at their disposal to eliminate nationalist militancy and republican sympathisers.
The Auxiliaries, or 'Auxies', quickly gained a well-merited reputation for drunkenness, brutality and summary justice. Their commander, Brig. Gen. Frank Crozier, resigned his command in February 1921 when he realised that he was powerless to discipline them.
The Auxiliaries were responsible for most of the terror that was unleashed on the Irish people, which earned the Black and Tans such a fearsome reputation.
The Black and Tans, in both of their manifestations, failed to break the resolve of the IRA, and they were disbanded, along with the RIC, following the Anglo-Irish Treaty in 1922.

Yeomanry

Yeomen were originally members of a part-time force established in 1796 as a local defence against the rising tide of nationalism and the United Irish movement, and also against the threat of invasion from France. They were mainly landowners and merchants loyal to the English administration in Ireland. By 1797 some 30,000 men had enlisted in the Yeomanry.
The vast majority of Yeomen were Protestants. They acted as vigilante groups against any formes of agrarian violence or manifestations of nationalistic sympathy. The force quickly gained a reputation for indiscipline and indiscriminate sectarian brutality.
They were particularly effective as a backup force for the English military during the 1798 Insurrection and it is speculated that the insurgents might well have been successful were it not for the Yeomen who were very familiar with their own locality and knew the identities of many of the local insurgents and were savage in their reprisals against any nationalist sympathisers.

After the 1798 Insurrection Yeomen were increasingly relied on as a local defence and security force, undertaking many of the duties formerly discharged by the English malitia. They also acted as an anti-invasion force during the Napoleonic War and their numbers reached a peak of 85,000 men in 1810.
Their significance gradually waned following the ending of the Napoleonic War in 1815, and in 1822 Yeomen ceased to be used for policing duties following the establishment of the Irish Constabulary, thus signalling a general decline in the movement. Yeomanry was formally disbanded in 1834
References to Yeomen are widespread in the 1798 ballads in this book.

Thomas Moore (1779 - 1852)

Thomas Moore was born in Dublin on May 28th, 1779, son of a shoemaker. He studied at Trinity College Dublin and was a close friend of Robert Emmet who led a small and abortive revolt in Dublin in 1803 and was executed as a result.
Moore was also acquainted with many of the United Irishmen and contributed to their newspaper, "The Press".
Combining his compositions with popular Irish airs of the period he published his works in the famous collections entitled "Irish Melodies", but now more popularly known as "Moore's Irish Melodies" or "Moore's Melodies". There were ten volumes, the first appearing in 1807 and the final one with a supplement appearing in 1834. The "Irish Melodies" were immensely popular in Ireland and Britain. The ten volumes contained 130 songs.
Moore in his "Irish Melodies" was seeking a richer and more sophisticated audience for Irish songs and the first volume was dedicated to "the Nobility and Gentry of Ireland". He was attempting to portray a more peaceful side to Irish Nationalism and his ballads are a far cry from the blood-thirsty and rabble-rousing ballads which proliferated the streets and ale houses in the early 19th century (samples of which are contained in this book - see pages 10, 28, and 52).
There were two distinctly different attitudes among Irish people towards Moore's ballads. Some considered that he had achieved more to awaken the nationalistic spirit of Irishmen than the rabble-rousing ballads more familiar to the Irish ear, while others regarded the "Irish Melodies" as whinging songs, bemoaning the downtrodden plight of Irish people while hanging from the coat-tails of the oppressor pleading for mercy.
Some of Moore's ballads were reprinted on street ballad broadsides in the middle years of the nineteenth century, particularly such songs as "Let Erin Remember" and "The Minstrel Boy".
There are two of Moore's ballads in this book:-
"The Harp That Once Through Tara's Halls" (page 5)
"The Minstrel Boy" (page 1)

Dublin Castle Main Gate
The headquarters of English and British administration in Ireland for over 800 years

The Minstrel Boy

A romantic ballad from the pen of Thomas Moore (1779 - 1852) and set to the old Irish tune "The Moreen".

See Additional Notes.

The Minstrel fell but the foeman's chain
Could not bring his proud soul under
The harp he loved never spoke again
For he tore its chords asunder
And said "No chains shall sully thee
Thou soul of love and bravery
Thy songs were made for the pure and free
They shall never sound in slavery"

The Minstrel Boy will return we pray
When we hear the news we all will cheer it
The Minstrel Boy will return one day
Torn perhaps in body, not in spirit
Then may he play on his harp in peace
In a world as heav'n intended
For all the bitterness of man must cease
And every battle must be ended.

MEMORIAL TO CHARLES STEWART PARNELL
Parnell Square, Dublin. See page 4

James Connolly

James Connolly (1868 - 1916) was a prominent labour leader and Irish rebel. He was born of Irish immigrant parents in Edinburgh in 1868. He was invited to Dublin in 1896 to establish the Irish Socialist Republican Party but he became disillusioned with the lack of popular support and enthusiasm for his socialist-republican ideals and he moved to the USA in 1903.

Connolly was invited back to Ireland in 1910 to run the newly established Socialist Party of Ireland. He was appointed Belfast organiser of the Irish Transport & General Workers' Union. In 1911 he established The Irish Textile Workers' Union and shortly after that was jailed for his part in the 1913 'Dublin lockout'.

He was a prominent political journalist and writer. His greatest works include "Labour in Irish History" (1910) and "The Re-Conquest of Ireland" (1915).

Connolly was a fervent advocate of Irish independence but was opposed to an imperialist rebellion as he felt that ordinary working people on both sides would suffer the greatest. He hoped that Germany would provide much needed assistance in an insurrection against British Rule in Ireland. His hopes were almost achieved but for an unfortunate communications blunder at Banna Strand in County Kerry. See "Banna Strand" - page 66.

In 1916, as Commandant of the Irish Citizen Army he formed an alliance with the leaders of the Irish Republican Brotherhood for a joint insurrection against British rule in Ireland. He fought in the 1916 Easter Rising, operating from the General Post Office in O'Connell Street, the headquarters for the Rising. He was one of the signatories on the Proclamation of the Irish Republic which was read by Padraig Pearse on the steps of the GPO. His ankle was shattered by a ricochet bullet on Easter Thursday.

My grand-uncle, Risteard Gogan, was one of his stretcher bearers as the insurgents evacuated the GPO on Friday April 28th.

James Connolly was condemned to death by court-martial for his part in the Rising. He was strapped to a chair and executed by firing squad in Kilmainham Jail, Dublin on May 12th, 1916.

For further information about the 1916 Rising see the Additional Notes.

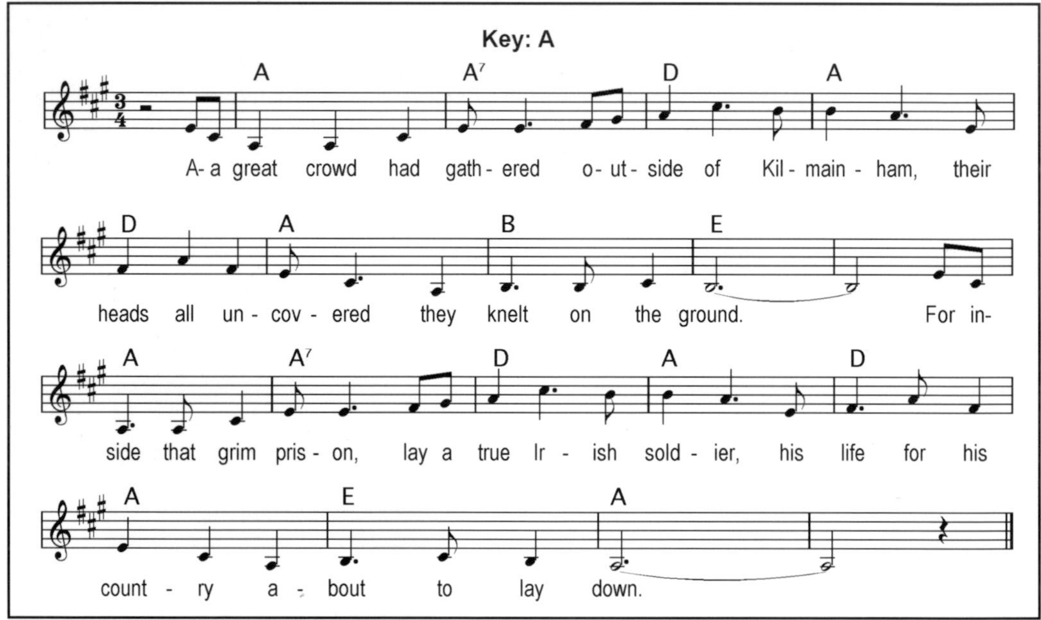

He went to his death like a true son of Erin
The firing party he bravely did face
Then the order rang out "Present arms" and "Fire!"
James Connolly fell into a ready made grave.

The black flag was hoisted, the cruel deed was over
Gone was the man who loved Ireland so well
There was many a sad heart in Dublin that morning
When they murdered James Connolly, the Irish rebel.

Many years have rolled by since the Irish Rebellion
When the guns of Britannia they loudly did speak
And the bold IRA they stood shoulder to shoulder
And the blood from their bodies flowed down Sackville Street.

The Four Courts of Dublin the English bombarded
The spirit of freedom they tried hard to quell
But above all the din came the cry "No Surrender!"
'Twas the voice of James Connolly, the Irish rebel.

The Four Courts, Dublin
Contains many of the State's courts, including the Supreme Court. In 1922 the building was occupied by the Anti-treaty forces. British artilliary was borrowed by the Irish Free State Army and the buildings were shelled, causing extensive damage.

Avondale

'Avondale', situated near Rathdrum in County Wicklow, was the family home of Charles Stewart Parnell (1846 - 1891). The house was built in 1777 for Samuel Hayes, a barrister who represented Wicklow in the Irish House of Commons, and was originally known as 'Hayesville'. Avondale passed to the Parnell family in 1795 and it was at Avondale on June 27th 1846 that Charles Stewart Parnell was born.

Parnell was one of Ireland's greatest Nationalist political leaders. As a Home Rule Member of Parliament for County Meath (1875 - 1880) and later for County Cork (1880 - 1891), he gained a reputation for his policy of obstructing the workings of the British Parliament. He was elected President of the Irish Land League and shortly after that, Chairman of the Irish Parliamentary Party. The general election of 1885, which elected 86 Nationalist Members of Parliament, was one of his greatest achievements.

He began to lose his influence following a bout of ill health and an affair with a married woman, Kitty O'Shea. At Mrs. O'Shea's divorce proceedings Parnell was cited as the 'co-respondent' and this led to a bitter split amongst Nationalist MP's. Many of his Irish supporters turned against him and the affair destroyed his career.

In June 1891 Parnell married Kitty O'Shea. He died in Brighton in the following October.

Many of his followers believe that it was through treachery and bribery that Parnell was cited in the divorce proceedings, hence the reference to "thirty pieces of silver" in the ballad.

Avondale is now a museum to Parnell's memory with many items relating to him and his life. There are also fine pieces of furniture original to the house and the Parnell family. The house was purchased by the State in 1904 and it was at Avondale that the first silvicultural experimental plots were laid out along the lines of a continental forest garden. The house and some 214 hectares of forest park are situated about 36 miles from South Dublin and are open to the public from about March to October each year - well worth a visit.

Many ballads have been written about Charles Stewart Parnell. Another very popular one is "The Blackbird of Sweet Avondale" written by his sister, Fanny Parnell, in 1881.

Where pride and ancient glory fade
So was the land where he was laid
Like Christ, was thirty pieces paid
For Avondale's proud eagle.

Long years that green and lovely vale
Has nursed Parnell, her proudest Gael
And cursed the land that has betrayed
Fair Avondale's proud eagle.
(Repeat first verse)

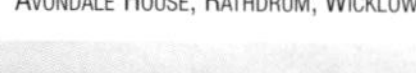
Avondale House, Rathdrum, Wicklow

The Harp That Once Through Tara's Halls

This is a ballad written by Thomas Moore (1779 - 1852) in which Moore uses symbolism to describe the sad state of Ireland under British rule. The harp is an ancient Irish musical instrument dating back over a thousand years. In this ballad it is used as a symbol of Irish spirit and freedom.

Indeed the harp was, and still is, an important symbol representing Ireland and 'Irishness'. The harp was central to both the flag of the United Irishmen in the 1790's and the Fenian Brotherhood in the 1860's. It also featured below the crown as the official symbol of British rule in Ireland. Today the harp is to be found on the notepaper of all official Irish Government communications and is used as the Irish symbol on all Irish Euro currency coins.

The Hill of Tara is a low-lying ridge situated in County Meath, in the east of Ireland. According to ancient traditions Tara was the seat of the High Kings of Ireland who controlled the northern half of the island. None of the structures has survived - they were all built of timber in ancient times - but the earthworks and ramparts which surrounded these dwellings, together with burial mounds, are still to be clearly seen.

Apart from the legends Tara is mentioned in many old annals and writings, so it certainly seems to have played an important part in early Irish history. Nobody knows how or why Tara fell into disuse or was abandoned.

To this day the name of Tara symbolises vanished splendour and glory.

For further details about Thomas Moore and his songs see the Additional Notes.

No more to chiefs and ladies bright the harp of Tara swells
The chord alone that breaks at night its tale of ruin tells
The freedom now so seldom wakes the only throb she gives
Is when some heart in sorrow breaks to show that still she lives.

Rotunda Assembly Rooms, Parnell Square, Dublin
At a mass meeting in this building the Irish Volunteers were formed in November 1913

The Rocky Road To Dublin

In Mullingar that night I rested limbs so weary
Started by daylight next morning bright and early
Took a drop o' the pure to keep me heart from sinking
That's a Paddy's cure when e'er he's on for drinking
See the lassies smile, laughing all the while
At my daring style, 'twould set your heart a-bubblin'
They asked if I was hired, what wages I required
Till I was almost tired of the rocky road to Dublin.
Chorus

In Dublin next arrived I thought it such a pity
To be so soon deprived a view of that fine city
When I took a stroll down among the quality
Me bundle it was stole in a neat locality
Something crossed me mind, then I looked behind
No bundle could I find on me stick a-wobblin'
Enquiring for the rogue, they said my Connaught brogue
Wasn't much in vogue on the rocky road to Dublin.
Chorus

From there I got away, me spirits never failing
Landed on the quay as the ship was sailing
Captain at me roared, said that no room had he
When I jumped aboard, a cabin found for Paddy
Down among the pigs I played some funny rigs
Danced some hearty jigs, the water 'round me bubblin'
When off Holyhead I wished meself was dead
Or better far instead, on the rocky road to Dublin.
Chorus

The boys of Liverpool when we safely landed
Called meself a fool, I could no longer stand it
Blood began to boil, temper I was losing
Poor old Erin's Isle they began abusing
"Hurrah, me boys!" says I, shillelagh I let fly
Some Galway boys were by and saw I was a-hobblin'
Then with loud "Hurray!" they joined in the affray
And quickly paved the way for the rocky road to Dublin.
Chorus

National War Memorial Park, Dublin
Dedicated to all Irish people who gave their lives
in the First and Second World Wars

God Save Ireland

On September 18th 1867 a band of Fenians attacked the police carriage transferring two Fenian prisoners, Col. Thomas J. Kelly and Timothy Deasy, from Belle Vue Jail to Borough Jail in Manchester.

In the skirmish a police sergeant, Charles Brett, was accidently shot dead.

Five men were sentenced to death for the killing (although only one shot was fired). Shortly afterward one of them, Thomas Maguire, was pardoned and a second, Edward O'Meagher Condon was reprieved owing to insufficient evidence. Many people expected that the case against the remaining three would be dropped. However, this was not to be so.

The remaining three were hanged on November 23rd 1867 - William Philip Allen, Michael Larkin and Michael O'Brien.

They quickly moved into Irish folklore and were revered as "The Manchester Martyrs".

The executions had an immediate impact on public opinion in Ireland and united all nationalists in their condemnation.

This ballad commemorates the bravery of the three men and was written by T.D. Sullivan. It was first published in 'The Nation' newspaper on December 7th, 1867.

The song is written to the George Root march "Tramp, Tramp, Tramp, the Boys are Marching", which was popular during the American Civil War.

In TD Sullivan's book "Recollections of Troubled Times In Irish Politics" Sullivan comments "Desirious of paying such tribute as I could to the memory of the patriots, I wrote, a few days after their execution, a song which had for its refrain the prayer which they had uttered in the docks, 'God Save Ireland'.

With a view to getting it into immediate use I fitted the words to a military air of American origin, 'Tramp, Tramp, Tramp, the Boys are Marching', which was popular at the time in Ireland. My intentions were fully realised; on the day of its publication in The Nation - December 7th, 1867 - it was sung in the homes of Dublin working men; on the following day I heard it sung and chorussed by a crowd of people in a railway station at Howth [Dublin]."

For further information on the Fenians and 'The Nation' see the Additional Notes

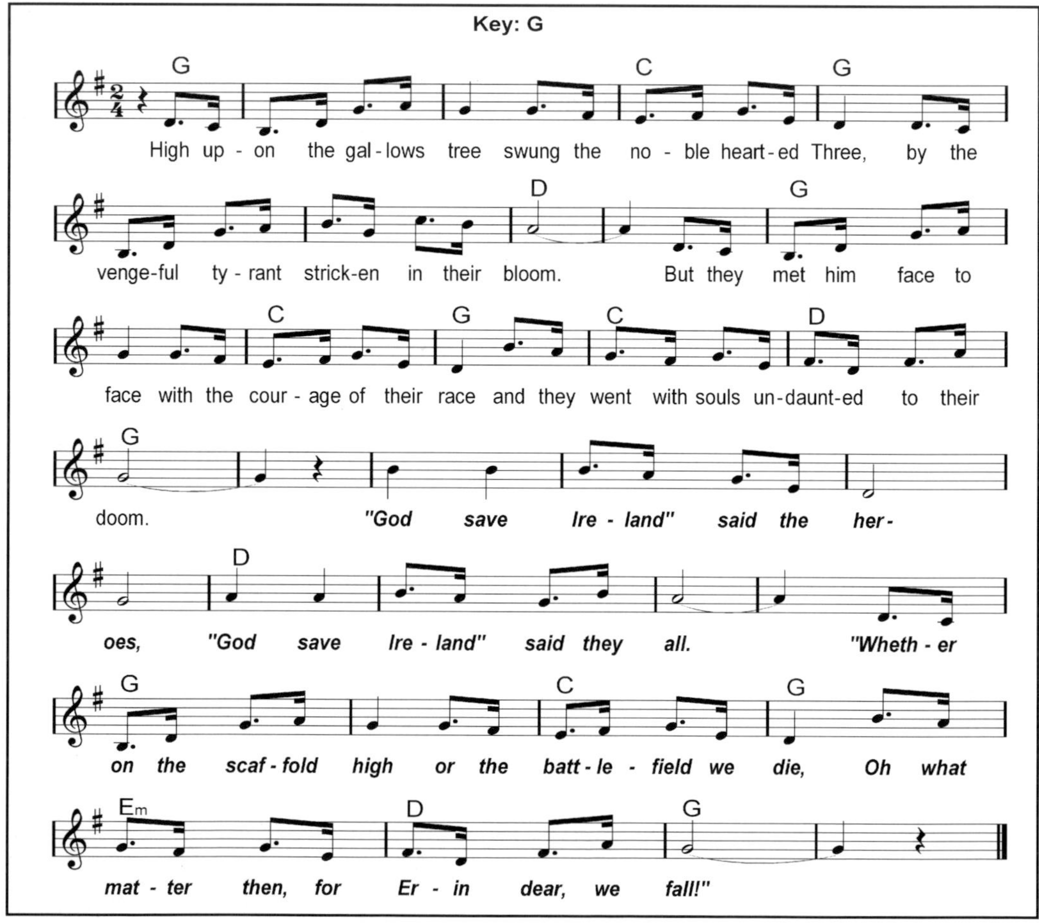

Girt around with cruel foes, still their spirit proudly rose
For they thought of hearts that loved them far and near
Of the millions true and brave o'er the ocean's swelling wave
And the friends in holy Ireland ever dear
Chorus change: "God save Ireland" said they proudly, etc.

Climbed they up the rugged stair, rung their voices out in prayer
Then with England's fatal cord around them cast
Close beneath the gallows tree, kissed like brothers lovingly
True to home and faith and freedom to the last
Chorus change: "God save Ireland" prayed they loudly, etc.

Never till the latest day shall the memory fade away
Of the gallant lives thus given for our land
But on the Cause must go amidst joy or weal or woe
Til we've made our isle a nation free and grand
Chorus change: "God save Ireland" say we proudly, etc.

Kilmainham Gaol, Dublin - Stonebreakers Yard
The cross marks the spot where the leaders of the 1916 Rebellion were executed by firing squad. (James Connolly was executed at the other end of the yard)

The Bold Fenian Men

This ballad was written by Michael Scanlan (1836 - 1900), who also wrote a well-known ballad entitled "The Jackets Green".

Scanlon was born in Castlemahon, County Limerick in 1833. During the Great Famine he left with his family for America. He joined the State Department in Washington where he eventually became the Chief of the Bureau of Statistics.

Along with other nationalist sympathisers Scanlan founded a newspaper called "The Irish Republic" in 1867, advocating and promoting the Fenian cause.

This is a rousing ballad and many's an Irishman saw the inside of a jail for the singing of it!

Sasanach is the Gaelic for Englishman and was usually uttered in a derogatory manner.

For further information on the Fenian Movement see the Additional Notes.

Our prayers and our tears have been scoffed and derided
They've shut out God's sunlight from spirit and mind
Our foes were united and we were divided
We met and they scattered our ranks to the wind
But once more returning; within our veins burning
The fires that illumined dark Aherlow Glen
We raise the cry anew; slogan of Conn and Hugh
Out and make way for the Bold Fenian Men

Up for the cause, then, fling forth our green banners
From the east to the west, from the south to the north
Irish land, Irish men, Irish mirth, Irish manners
From the mansion and the cot let the slogan go forth
Sons of old Ireland now; Love you our sireland now?
Come from the kirk or the chapel or glen
Down with the faction old; concert and action bold
This is the creed of the Bold Fenian Men

We've men from the North, from the Suir and the Shannon
Let the tyrants come forth, we'll bring force against force
Our pen is the sword and our voice is the cannon
Rifle for rifle and horse against horse
We've made the false Saxon yield many a red battlefield
God on our side we will triumph again
Pay them back woe for woe; Give them back blow for blow
Out and make way for the bold Fenian Men

Side by side for the cause have our forefathers battled
When our hills never echoed the tread of a slave
In many a field where the leaden hail rattled
Through the red gap of glory they marched to the grave
And those who inherit their name and their spirit
Will march 'neath the banners of Liberty then
All who love foreign law, native or Sasanach
Must out and make way for the Bold Fenian Men.

Poster on a wall at Parnell Square, Dublin

Bold Thady Quill

(The chorus is similar to the melody of the first four lines of the verse)

This ballad is popular throughout Ireland but particularly in County Cork. The air is also used in another Irish ballad, "Killeadan".

Duhallow is situated along the Cork and Kerry borders in the south of Ireland and is comprised of the ancient Baronies of Duhallow, West Muskerry and parts of East Kerry. There are three main market towns in the district - Kanturk, Millstreet and Newmarket, together with a number of small villages

Banteer is a village and townland in Duhallow about three miles from Kanturk and athletic competitions used to be held there each year. Athletes gathered from far and wide at these games which were well known and very popular. Dr. Pat O'Callaghan (1905 - 1991) who came from Duhallow, was the first athlete to win Olympic gold medals for Ireland, in 1928 and 1932, on both occasions in the hammer-throwing competition. No doubt he probably took part in the Banteer Games at some stage!

It is reputed that Thady Quill was no athlete at all, but a lazy farm worker employed by a farmer named Johnny Tom Gleeson in Ballinagree (a townland in Muskerry). The local story goes that Johnny Tom Gleeson penned these verses as a satire to Thady's laziness and inactivity. At least that's the legend anyway!

'Parnell' is a reference to Charles Stewart Parnell a nationalist and leader of the Irish Parliamentary Party who died in 1891. See "Avondale" - page 4.

'Hurling', of course, is one of our two most popular national games in Ireland (Gaelic Football being the other). It is particularly strong in the southern counties and there has been many's a passionate hurling match over the years between Cork and Tipperary!

For rambling, for roving, for football or sporting, for emptying a bowl just as fast as you'd fill
In all your days roving you'll find none so jovial as the Muskerry sportsman, the bold Thady Quill

Now Thady was famous in all sorts of places; at the athletic meeting held out in Cloughroe
He won the long jump without throwin' off his braces; goin' fifty-four feet, leppin' off from the toe
And at throwing the weight was a Dublinman foremost; but Thady outreached and exceeded him still
And 'round the whole field went the wide ringing chorus; "Here's luck to our hero, the bold Thady Quill!"
Chorus

At the great hurling match between Cork and Tipp'rary; 'twas played in the Park by the banks of the Lee
Our own darling boys were afraid of being beaten; so they sent for bold Thady to Ballinagree
He hurled the ball left and right into their faces; and showed the Tipp'rary boys learning and skill
If they came in his way he was willing to brain them; the papers were full of the praise of Thade Quill.
Chorus

In the year '91 before Parnell was taken; our Thade was outrageously breaking the peace
He got a light sentence for causing commotion; and six months hard labour for beating police
But in spite of coercion he's still agitating; ev'ry drop of his life's blood he's willing to spill
To gain for old Ireland complete liberation; till then there's no rest for the bold Thady Quill.
Chorus

At the Cork Exhibition there was a fair lady; whose fortune exceeded a million or more
But a bad constitution had ruined her completely; and medical treatment had failed o'er and o'er
"Oh mother", she said, "sure I know what'll cure me; and all my diseases most certainly kill
Give over your doctors and medical treatment; I'd rather one squeeze from the bold Thady Quill!"
Chorus

Banteer post office and crossroads, Cork

Lanigan's Ball

Athy is a town in County Kildare, in the east of Southern Ireland, about 40 miles from Dublin.
'Punch' is a very potent alcoholic drink served from a large bowl and is very popular at Irish parties. There can be several varieties of alcoholic drink mixed into the formula which can differ according to the tastes of its maker.
Naturally punch can be very potent! Because of its sweet taste and mulled properties there is a tendency to drink it quickly and in large amounts. Before you know where you are it can creep up on you and give you one hell of a wallop - hence the name! You've been warned - watch out!

Meself to be sure got free invitations for all the nice colleens and boys I might ask
Just in a minute both friends and relations were dancing as merry as bees 'round a cask
There was lashings of punch, wine for the ladies; potatoes and cakes, there was bacon and tay
There were the Nolans, the Dolans, O'Gradys courting the girls and dancing away

They were doing all kinds of nonsensical polkas all 'round the room in a whirligig
Till Julie and I soon banished their nonsense and tipped them a twist of a real Irish jig
O how that girl she got mad and we danced till we thought that the ceilings would fall
For I spent three weeks at Brook's Academy learning to dance for Lanigan's Ball. ***Chorus***

The boys were all merry, the girls all hearty dancing together in couples and groups
Till an accident happened, young Terence McCarthy; he put his right leg through Miss Finnerty's hoops
The creature she fainted and called "melia murder"; called for her brothers and gathered them all
Carmody swore that he'd go no further; he'd get satisfaction at Lanigan's Ball.

In the midst of the row Miss Kerrigan fainted; her cheeks at the same time as red as a rose
Some of the boys decreed she was painted; she took a small drop too much I suppose
Her sweetheart Ned Morgan so powerful and able; when he saw his fair colleen stretched by the wall
He tore the left leg from under the table and smashed all the dishes at Lanigan's Ball. ***Chorus***

Boys, O boys 'tis then there was ructions; I took a leg from young Phelim McHugh
But soon I replied to his fine introductions and kicked him a terrible hullabaloo
Old Casey the piper he nearly got strangled; they squeezed up his pipes, bellows, chanters and all
The girls in their ribbons they all got entangled and that put an end to Lanigan's Ball. ***Chorus***

James Larkin Statue, O'Connell Street, Dublin
Larkin was a labour leader during the notorious 'Dublin Lockout' of 1913, which directly led to the formation of the Irish Citizen Army

Finnegan's Wake

This is a very popular Dublin ballad. Tim Finnegan lived in "Watling Street" which is situated in the heart of Dublin city not far from the famous Guinness brewery at James Gate. In the ballad Tim is a builder's labourer who is rather fond of booze.

Some versions of this ballad have Tim Finnegan living in "Walkin Street" but I can't find a Walkin Street in Dublin anywhere!
James Joyce took the title of this ballad for his final book "Finnegans Wake".

Key: C

C Am F
Tim Finn- eg - an lived in Wat- ling Street, a gen - tle - man Ir - ish

G7 C Am
might- y odd. He had a brogue both rich and sweet, and to

F G7 C
rise in the world he carr - ied a hod. Tim had a bit of a

Am C Am
tip - pl - in' way. With the love of the liq - uor he was born. And to

C Am F
send him on his way each day a drop of the creath - ur*

G7 C Am
ev - ery morn. ***Whack fol - de - da, will you dance with your part- ner a-***

F G7 C
round the floor your trot - ters shake. Is - n't it the

Am F G7 C
truth I told ye, lots of fun at Finn - eg - an's wake!

One morning Tim was rather full; his head felt heavy which made him shake
He fell off the ladder and he broke his skull and they carried him home his corpse to wake
They wrapped him up in a nice clean sheet and they laid him out upon the bed
With a bottle of whiskey at his feet and a barrel of porter at his head. ***Chorus***

His friends assembled at the wake and Mrs. Finnegan called for lunch
First she gave them tay and cake, then piped tobacco and brandy punch
Then the Widow Malone began to cry; such a lovely corpse she did ever see
"Yerra Tim mo bhourneen** why did you die"; "Will you hold your hour" said Molly Magee. ***Chorus***

Then Mary Murphy took up the job; "Yerra Biddy" says she "You're wrong, I'm sure"
Then Biddy fetched her a belt in the gob and left her sprawling on the floor
Civil war did then engage; woman to woman and man to man
Shillelagh law was all the rage and a row and a ruction soon began. ***Chorus***

Tim Moloney ducked his head when a bottle of whiskey flew at him
He ducked and, landing on the bed, the whiskey scattered over Tim
Well begob he revives and see how he's rising; Tim Finnegan rising in the bed
Saying "Fling your whiskey 'round like blazes! Be the thundering Jayses d'ye think I'm dead!" ***Chorus***

*Booze - usually whiskey
** Pronounced 'mo vourneen' (my loved one)

Watling Street, Dublin

Whiskey In The Jar

I have come across many different versions of this ballad with equally as many changes of location and character names! This was always a very popular Irish ballad and was made even more so by a recording of a modern version of it by the Irish rock legend, Phil Lynott (now, sadly, no longer with us), and his band Thin Lizzy. It was a major hit for them back in 1973.

I counted out his money and it made a pretty penny
I put it in my pocket and I brought it home to Jenny
She sighed and she vowed that she never would deceive me
But the devil take the women for they never can be easy. ***Chorus***

I went into her chamber all for to take a slumber
I dreamt of gold and jewels and for sure it was no wonder
But Jenny took my pistols and she filled them full of water
And sent for Captain Farrell to be ready for the slaughter. ***Chorus***

'Twas early in the morning just before I rose to travel
The redcoats stood around the bed and likewise Captain Farrell
I then produced my pistols for she stole away my rapier
I couldn't shoot with water so a prisoner I was taken. ***Chorus***

They threw me into prison, bound without a writ or bounty
For robbin' Captain Farrell near the Cork and Kerry mountains
But they couldn't take me fist so I punched and knocked the sentry
And bade no farewell to the Captain or the gentry. ***Chorus***

If I could find my brother who is listed in the army
I know that he would rescue me in Cork or in Killarney
We'd set out from this place and go roving in Kilkenny
I'd be much safer there than beside my faithless Jenny. ***Chorus***

Some men delight in fishing, others they like bowling
Some men like the fields or the sea that goes a-rolling
But me I take my pleasures in the juice of the barley
And not courting pretty maidens in the morning bright and early. ***Chorus***

Children Of Lir Memorial
Situated in the Garden Of Remembrance, Parnell Square, Dublin. The Garden, opened in 1966, is a memorial to those who died throughout the course of Irish history in the struggle for Irish independence

The Rising Of The Moon

The lyrics for this song were written in 1865 by John Keegan Casey (1846 - 1870) to the melody of "The Wearing Of The Green" (page 54). The subject matter of the ballad is the action in County Longford during the 1798 Rebellion.

About 6,000 men assembled near Granard in County Longford on September 4th 1798. They were led by two brothers, Hans and Alexander Denniston, and they attacked Granard. However the attack quickly turned into a massacre and many of the insurgents fled. The English garrison of 250 Yeomen under the command of a Major Porter killed over 400 insurgents, with only two men wounded on the English side.

It is understood that Casey's original draft of the first line in the fourth verse was "There beside the Inny River..." However, not wanting to bring too much attention from the British to his own local area he changed the line to its present form.

Casey came from Milltown, Rathconrath, near the town of Mullingar in County Westmeath, in the east-midlands of Ireland. He was the son of a small farmer and was imprisoned at the age of twenty for his support of the Fenians, a revolutionary nationalist movement which was established in Ireland in the mid 19th century. When released from prison he worked as a journalist in Dublin and was a regular contributor to "The Nation" newspaper, under the pseudonym "Leo". He died as a result of a traffic accident on O'Connell Bridge in Dublin in 1870 and an enormous crowd attended his funeral.

Along with "Boulavogue" (page 68) this ballad is one of the most popular anthems of the 1798 Rebellion.

For further information about the 1798 Rebellion see the Additional Notes.

"Oh then tell me Sean O'Farrell where the gathering's to be"
"In the old spot by the river, right well known to you and me
One word more - for signal token, whistle up the marching tune
With your pike upon your shoulder by the rising of the moon"
By the rising of the moon, by the rising of the moon
With your pike upon your shoulder by the rising of the moon.

Out of many a mud-wall cabin eyes were watching out that night
Many a manly heart was throbbing for that blessed warning light
Murmurs passed along the valley like a banshee's lonely croon
And a thousand blades were flashing at the rising of the moon
At the rising of the moon, at the rising of the moon
And a thousand blades were flashing at the rising of the moon.

There beside that singing river that dark mass of men was seen
Far above the shining weapons hung their own beloved green
"Death to every foe and traitor! Forward! Strike the marching tune
And hurrah, me boys, for freedom! 'Tis the rising of the moon"
'Tis the rising of the moon, 'tis the rising of the moon
And hurrah, me boys, for freedom 'tis the rising of the moon.

Well they fought for dear old Ireland and full bitter was their fate
(Oh what glorious pride and sorrow fills the name of "Ninety-Eight")
Yet thank God e'en still are beating hearts in manhood's burning noon
Who would follow in their footsteps at the rising of the moon
At the rising of the moon, at the rising of the moon
Who would follow in their footsteps at the rising of the moon.

*Pronounced "voukill" (boy)

Croppies' Acre, Dublin
Mass burial ground for insurgents of the 1798 Rebellion, situated on the quays in the centre of Dublin

The Banks Of My Own Lovely Lee

This Cork anthem is a popular ballad which every self-respecting Cork person would happily sing at the drop of a hat and is affectionately known throughout Cork as 'The Banks'. The Lee is the principle river of County Cork. It rises in Lake Gougane Barra and flows through the centre of Cork City in the south of Ireland out to the sea. The promenade of the "Mardyke" is at its centre but the elm trees are long gone. The "banks" referred to in the ballad extend westward along the Lee fields to Inishcarra and eastwards towards the harbour down the Marina to Blackrock.

And then in the springtime of laughter and song; can I ever forget the sweet hours
With the friends of my youth as we rambled along; 'mongst the green mossy banks and wild flowers
Then too, when the evening's sun sinking to rest; sheds its golden light over the sea
The maid with her lover the wild daisies pressed; on the banks of my own lovely Lee
Yes the maid with her lover wild daisies they pressed; on the banks of my own lovely Lee.

'Tis a beautiful land this dear isle of song; its gems shed their light on the world
And her faithful sons bore thro' ages of wrong; the banner St. Patrick unfurled
Oh, would I were there with the friends I love best; and my fond bosom partner with me
We'd roam thy bank over and when weary we'd rest; by thy waters, my own lovely Lee
Yes we'd roam thy banks over and when weary we'd rest; by thy waters, my own lovely Lee.

Oh what joys should be mine e're this life should decline; to seek shells on thy sea-gilded shore
While the steel-feathered eagle, oft splashing the brine; brings longing for freedom once more
Oh all that upon earth I wish for or crave; that my last crimson drop be for thee
To moisten the grass on my forefathers' grave; on the banks of my own lovely Lee
Yes to moisten the grass on my forefathers' grave; on the banks of my own lovely Lee.

(Verses and chorus have the same melody)

This ballad is a parody of the English Song "The Jolly Ploughboy" which is a song in praise of the British soldier's way of life.
It is an obvious rebel song, where the singer is tired of oppression and has decided to join the I.R.A. In the English version, the singer joins the R.H.A. - the Royal Horse Artillery. "I.R.A." refers to the Irish Republican Army. The I.R.A. evolved out of the former Irish Volunteer movement which played such a prominent role in the 1916 Easter Rising. After the foundation of Dáil Eireann in 1919 the I.R.A. began to be accepted as the armed force which would be employed to remove British rule from Ireland.
The I.R.A. fought on the anti-Treaty side in the Civil War (1922-1923) and was defeated. However the remnants of the organisation refused to recognise the subsequent Irish Free State or the legitimacy of Northern Ireland.
The I.R.A. has survived to the present day albeit in various different splinter groups and formats.

So I'm off to Dublin in the green, in the green; where the helmets glisten in the sun
Where the bayonets flash and the rifles crash; to the echo of a Thompson gun.

I'll leave aside my pick and spade, I'll leave aside my plough
I'll leave aside my old grey mare for no more I'll need them now. ***Chorus***

And I'll leave aside my Mary, she's the girl that I adore
And I wonder if she'll think of me when she hears the cannons roar
And when the war is over, and dear old Ireland's free
I will take her to the church to wed and a rebel's wife she'll be. ***Chorus***

AUGHRIM, GALWAY
Mural celebrating the Battle of Aughrim 1691, fought between the forces of the Jacobites and Williamites.
The Williamites were victorious and over 7,000 fleeing Jacobites were slaughtered

O'Donnell Abú

"Abú" is an abbreviation for the Irish war cry "Go Bua!" ("To Victory!").

This ballad was written by Michael Joseph McCann (1824 - 1883), a native of County Galway. It first appeared in 'The Nation' newspaper in 1843 under the title "The Clanconnell War Song".

The subject matter of the ballad is 'Red Hugh' O'Donnell (1572 - 1602), Lord of Tirconnell from 1592, and his defeat of the English forces under Sir Conyers Clifford at Ballyshannon, Co. Donegal (north-west of Ireland) in 1597.

"Saimer" is the ancient name for the districts around Ballyshannon.

When O'Donnell was betrothed to the daughter of Hugh O'Neill, Earl of Tyrone, the English feared the establishment of a strong Irish alliance in the Northern part of Ireland and consequently O'Donnell was arrested and imprisoned in Dublin Castle. After four years, and on his second attempt, he escaped from Dublin Castle with the connivance of O'Neill. During the Nine Years War the capture of Sligo Castle allowed O'Donnell to exercise authority over most of North Connaught.

"Bonnaught" and "Gallowglass" are references to the use of mercenary troops which was widespread in Ireland during the 16th and 17th centuries.

When Spanish forces landed in Kinsale in 1601 O'Donnell marched his army down to Munster to join with them. Evading the English forces with a brilliant flanking manoeuvre at Cashel, County Tipperary, he and the Irish armies arrived successfully in Kinsale but were defeated at the Battle of Kinsale (1601). He then sailed to Spain to seek further assistance for the Irish Cause but died there.

Princely O'Neill to our aid is advancing
With many a chieftain and warrior clan
A thousand proud steeds in his vanguard are prancing
'Neath Borderers brave from the banks of the Bann
Many a heart shall quail under its coat of mail
Deeply the merciless foeman shall rue
When on his ear shall ring, borne on the breeze's wing
Tir Connell's dread war cry "O'Donnell Abú!"

Wildly o'er Desmond the war-wolf is howling
Fearless the eagle sweeps over the plain
The fox in the streets of the city is prowling
And all who would scare them are banished or slain
Grasp, every stalwart hand, hackbut and battle-brand
Pay them all back the deep debt so long due
Norris and Clifford well can of Tir Connell tell
Onward to glory, O'Donnell Abú!

Sacred the cause that Clan Connell's defending
The alters we kneel at, the homes of our sires
Ruthless the ruin the foe is extending
Midnight is red with the plunderer's fires
On with O'Donnell then, fight the old fight again
Sons of Tir Connell all valiant and true
Make the false Saxon feel Erin's avenging steel
Strike for your country, O'Donnell Abú!

Battle of the Boyne, 1690
Oldbridge, Meath, scene of the Battle of the Boyne fought in these fields between the forces of William III and James II. The Williamites were victorious

The Foggy Dew

This ballad was written by an Irish priest, Canon Charles O'Neill, as a tribute to the men and women who fought against the British in the Easter Rising of 1916.

In 1919 Canon O'Neill attended the first sitting of the Irish Parliament (Dáil Eireann). He was taken aback by the number of members at roll-call who were described as "faoi ghlas ag na Gaill" (locked up by the foreigners) and was moved by emotion to write this ballad.

References in the ballad are made to Suvla Bay (Gallipoli) and Sud-el-Bar (Mesopotamia) - two battles in which many Irishmen gave their lives while serving in the British Army during the First World War.

There was an expectation among the leaders of the Rising that the British authorities would never use heavy artillery to bombard Dublin which was considered at the time to be the 'Second City' of the British Empire after London. However the insurgents were very much mistaken. Extensive use of artillery by the British laid waste large areas of the city centre - the "great big guns" referred to in the ballad.

In the ballad, reference is made to "Pearse" - Padraig Pearse, one of the leaders of the Rising; "Cathal Brugha" - one of the heroes who was badly injured during the fighting at the South Dublin Union; "Albion" - ancient name for the island of Great Britain; "Wild Geese" - a term applied to Irish patriots who were forced to flee Ireland in the 17th and 18th centuries, many of whom distinguished themselves in foreign armies; "Fenian" - a revolutionary Nationalist movement of the mid 19th century.

For further information about the Easter Rising see the Additional Notes.

Right proudly high in Dublin town they hoisted up the flag of war
'Twas better to die 'neath an Irish sky that at Suvle or Sud el Bar
And from the plains of Royal Meath strong men came hurrying through
While Brittania's Huns with their great big guns sailed in through the foggy dew.

Oh the night fell black and the rifles' crack made "Perfidious Albion" reel
'Mid the leaden rain seven tongues of flame did shine o'er the lines of steel
By each shining blade a prayer was said that to Ireland her sons be true
When the morning broke still the war flag shook out its folds in the foggy dew.

'Twas England made our Wild Geese flee so that small nations might be free
But their lonely graves are by Suvla's waves or the fringe of the Great North Sea
Oh had they died by Pearse's side or had fought with Cathal Brugha
Their names we would keep where the Fenians sleep 'neath the shroud of the foggy dew.

But the bravest fell and the requiem bell rang out mournfully and clear
For those who died that Easter tide in the springtime of the year
While the world did gaze with deep amaze at those fearless men, but few
Who bore the fight that Freedom's light might shine through the foggy dew.

Ah! back through the glen I rode again and my heart with grief was sore
For I parted then with valiant men whom I never will see no more
But to and fro in my dreams I go and I kneel and pray for you
For slavery fled, O glorious dead, when you fell in the foggy dew.

Kilmainham Gaol
West wing, first floor landing. It was in these cells that the leaders of the 1916 Rebellion were held before their execution in the stonebreakers yard

The Boys Of Wexford

(The melody of the chorus is similar to the last two lines of the verse)

This ballad is another popular anthem emanating from the 1798 Rebellion, and, as a lively march, has always been included in the repertoire of Irish Army bands.

There are two versions of this song. The original version was written by Robert Dwyer Joyce to a diferent tune. There were references in the original ballad to the curse of drink, and it reflected the prevailing loyalist view that the 1798 insurgents were nothing more than a drunken unruly mob. This song was first published in 'The Irish People' in 1863.

A revised version of the ballad, the one below, used most of Joyce's lyrics but omitting the references to alcohol. It was compiled by Edmund Leamy and first published in "Songs of the Gael" (1922) edited by Fr. Padraig Breathnach with an introduction that it was 'an improvement on the old song by Dr. Robert Dwyer Joyce'.

The air to which the song is now sung is to be found in "Ancient Music of Ireland from the Petrie Collection" (1877).

Robert Dwyer Joyce was a nationalist, born in County Limerick in 1830. He graduated as a doctor in 1865 and left Ireland following the failure of the Fenian Rising of that year. He practised medecine in Boston and returned to Dublin in 1883 and died the same year.

Lord Mountjoy (second verse) was the Colonel of the Dublin Regiment who was killed at the Three-Bullet Gate during the battle of New Ross (5th June 1798).

The third verse refers to the Battle of Tubberneering (4th June 1798) at which Colonel Lambert was killed and his company wiped out by the insurgents.

'Forth' and 'Shelmalier' are districts in Wexford, also referred to in "Kelly From Killane" (page 60). 'Oulart' refers to the battle of Oulart (27th May 1798) a significant victory for the insurgents.

'Vinegar Hill' refers to the Battle of Vinegar Hill (21st June 1798) at which the insurgents were decisively beaten, thus ending the Wexford corridore of the 1798 Rebellion.

For further information on the 1798 Rebellion see the Additional Notes.

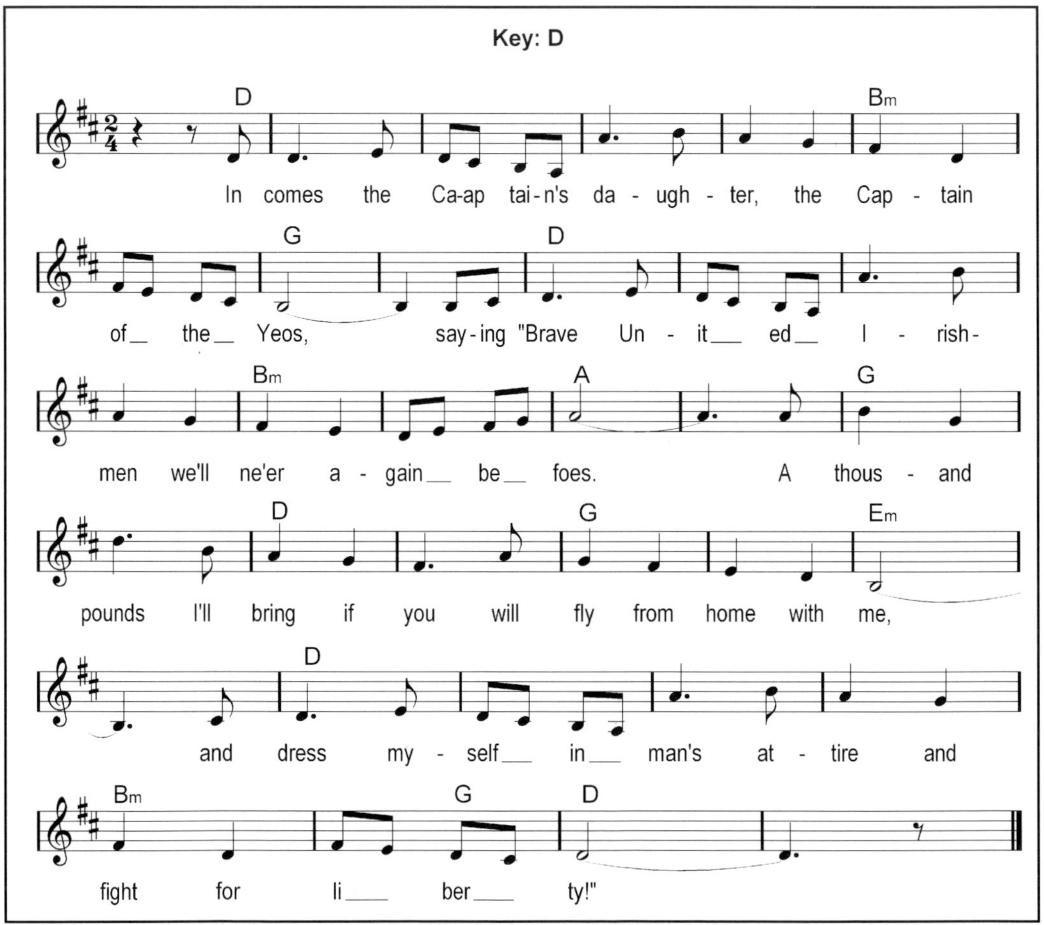

We are the Boys of Wexford, who fought with heart and hand
To burst in twain the galling chain and free our native land

I want no gold, my maiden fair, to fly from home with thee
Your shining eyes will be my prize, more dear than gold to me
I want no gold to nerve my arm to do a true man's part
To free my land I'd gladly give the red drops from my heart.
Chorus

And when we left our cabins boys we left with right good will
To see our friends and neighbours that were at Vinegar Hill
A young man from our ranks, a cannon he let go
He slapt it into Lord Mountjoy, a tyrant he laid low!
Chorus

We bravely fought and conquered at Ross and Wexford Town
Three-Bullet Gate, for years to come, will speak for our renown
Through Walpole's horse and Walpole's foot on Tubberneering's day
Depending on the long bright pike we cut our gory way!
Chorus

And Oulart's name shall be their shame, whose steel we ne'er did fear
For every man could do his part like Forth and Shelmalier
And if for want of leaders we lost at Vinegar Hill
We're ready for another fight and love our country still!
Chorus

Ballinglen Bridge, Wicklow

Brennan On The Moor

This ballad first appeared on a broadside printed by Haly of Cork in 1850.

The central character is a highwayman called Willie Brennan who carried on his 'trade' at the beginning of the 19th century. He spent most of his time in and around the Kilworth Mountains, between the towns of Mitchelstown and Fermoy in County Cork in the south of Ireland. The main road between Dublin and Cork crosses over the Kilworth Mountains.

Highwaymen were also known as 'tories' or 'rapparees' and were regarded as champions of the poor and downtrodden. Many of these men were respectable or semi-respectable Catholic landowners who were dispossessed of their lands in the 17th century and who waged a war of revenge against the new social order. The early rapparees sheltered in the woods, mountains and boglands and waged a type of guerrilla war against the authorities and against those who had seized their lands. Rapparee activity remained widespread throughout Ireland in the troubled years immediately following the Williamite War (1689 - 1691) and continued into the 18th century in South Ulster and in parts of the south-west.

Many fine ballads have been written about these highwaymen whose daring and heroic deeds and scornful regard for the authorities and the Law endeared them to the common people. Ballads were even written about Irish rapparees who travelled abroad to carry on their trade . See "The Wild Colonial Boy" - page 44.

There was a ballad popular around the borders of Kansas and Missouri in America sung to the same air as this song and with remarkably similar words and phrases. It was entitled "Charlie Quantrell-O" and the subject of the ballad was an outlaw by the name of William Clarke Quantrell (whose nickname was 'Charlie Quantrell') who was causing a lot of trouble for the authorities around Kansas and Missouri in the 1860's.

Cashel is a town situated in County Tipperary, not far from Mitchelstown and the Kilworth Mountains.

Willie Brennan was arrested and hanged in 1804.

A brace of loaded pistols he carried night and day
He never robbed a poor man upon the broad highway
But what he'd taken from the rich, and nothing more or less
He always did divide it with the people in distress.

Chorus - As did Brennan on the Moor, etc.

One day upon the highway as Willie he went down
He met the Mayor of Cashel a mile outside the town
The mayor he knew his features, "I think young man" said he
"Your name is Willie Brennan, you must come along with me".
Chorus - And it's Brennan on the Moor, etc.

Now Brennan's wife had gone to town, provisions for to buy
And when she saw her Willie she began to weep and cry
She said "Hand me that tenpenny" as soon as Willie spoke
She handed him a blunderbuss from underneath her cloak.
Chorus - For young Brennan on the Moor, etc.

Then with his loaded blunderbuss the truth I will unfold
He made the mayor to tremble and robbed him of his gold
One hundred pounds was offered for his apprehension there
So he with horse and saddle to the mountains did repair.
Chorus - Did young Brennan on the Moor, etc.

Now Brennan being an outlaw and upon the mountain high
With cavalry and infantry to take him they did try
He laughed at them with scorn until at last as it was said
By a false-hearted woman he was cruelly betrayed.
Chorus - Was young Brennan on the Moor, etc.

When Brennan and his comrades they knew they were betrayed
They with the mounted cavalry a noble battle made
Then Willie's foremost finger was shot off by a ball
And Willie and his comrades they were taken one and all.
Chorus - Was young Brennan on the Moor, etc.

When Brennan heard his sentence this was his bold reply
"I owe that I did rob the rich and did the poor supply
In all the deeds that I have done I took no life away
The Lord have mercy on my soul against the Judgement Day!"
Chorus - Said young Brennan on the Moor, etc.

They put a rope around his neck, in chains he swung and died
But still they say on winter nights bold Brennan he doth ride
They say that with his blunderbuss all in the midnight chill
Across the Kilworth Mountains rides bold Willie Brennan still!
Chorus - Does young Brennan on the Moor, etc.

"In order to prevent the further slaughter of Dublin citizens, and in the hope of saving the lives of our followers now surrounded and hopelessly outnumbered, the members of the Provisional Government present at Headquaters have agreed to an unconditional surrender, and the Commandants of the various districts in the City and Country will order their commands to lay down arms.

(Signed) P.H. Pearse
29th April, 1916, 3.45pm"

Instrument of surrender issued by Padraic Pearse following the failed 1916 Rebellion

Johnny I Hardly Knew Ye

(Versus and chorus have the same melody)

This anti war ballad is very similar to another song called "When Johnny Comes Marching Home" which was written by the U.S. Union Army bandmaster Patrick Gilmore in 1863 and was a ballad glorifying army life. Nobody seem to know which song came first!
The reference to Ceylon (Sulloon) may help to date the ballad. The British occupied Ceylon from 1796 to 1948. During that period there were three rebellions for independence - 1817, which was quite serious, and two minor outbreaks in 1843 and 1848. 'Johnny' in the ballad could have been injured in one of these rebellions. Or he may have been struck down by sickness and disease which was rampant among the occupying forces in Ceylon the 19th century.
Athy is a town in County Kildare.

With your drums and guns and guns and drums Ha-roo, Ha-roo
With your drums and guns and guns and drums Ha-roo, Ha-roo
With your drums and guns and guns and drums the enemy nearly slew ye
My darling dear you look so queer, Johnny I hardly knew ye!

Where are your eyes that looked so mild Ha-roo, Ha-roo
Where are your eyes that looked so mild Ha-roo, Ha-roo
Where are your eyes that looked so mild when my poor heart you first beguiled
Why did you run from me and the child, Johnny I hardly knew ye. ***Chorus***

Where are the legs with which you run Ha-roo, Ha-roo
Where are the legs with which you run Ha-roo, Ha-roo
Where are the legs with which you run when you went off to carry a gun
Indeed your dancing days are done, Johnny I hardly knew ye. ***Chorus***

It grieved my heart to see you sail Ha-roo, Ha-roo
It grieved my heart to see you sail Ha-roo, Ha-roo
It grieved my heart to see you sail though from my heart you took leg-bail
Like a cod you're doubled up head and tail, Johnny I hardly knew ye. ***Chorus***

You haven't an arm you haven't a leg Ha-roo, Ha-roo
You haven't an arm you haven't a leg Ha-roo, Ha-roo
You haven't an arm you haven't a leg you're an eyeless, noseless, chickenless egg
You'll have to be put in a bowl to beg, Johnny I hardly knew ye. ***Chorus***

I'm happy for to see you home Ha-roo, Ha-roo
I'm happy for to see you home Ha-roo, Ha-roo
I'm happy for to see you home all from the island of Sulloon
So low in flesh so high in bone, Johnny I hardly knew ye. ***Chorus***

But sad as it is to see you so Ha-roo, Ha-roo
But sad as it is to see you so Ha-roo, Ha-roo
But sad as it is to see you so I think of you now as an object of woe
Your Peggy'll still keep you on as her beau, Johnny I hardly knew ye. ***Chorus***

Castlebar, Mayo
Memorial to the 1798 Rebellion

Mrs. McGrath

This song dates from around 1815, the era of the Peninsular Wars. The earliest account of it in Ireland is 1876 but it was also popular during the American Civil War.
It was a favourite marching song of the Irish Volunteers between 1913 and 1916.
The identity of 'Don John' is unknown but the reference to the King of Spain probably refers to Joseph Bonaparte (brother of Napoleon) who had been installed as the Spanish monarch in 1808.
Other anti-recruiting ballads in this book are "The Kerry Recruit" (page 38) and "Johnny, I Hardly Knew Ye!" (page 32).
Many's an Irishman saw the inside of a jail for the singing of these songs!

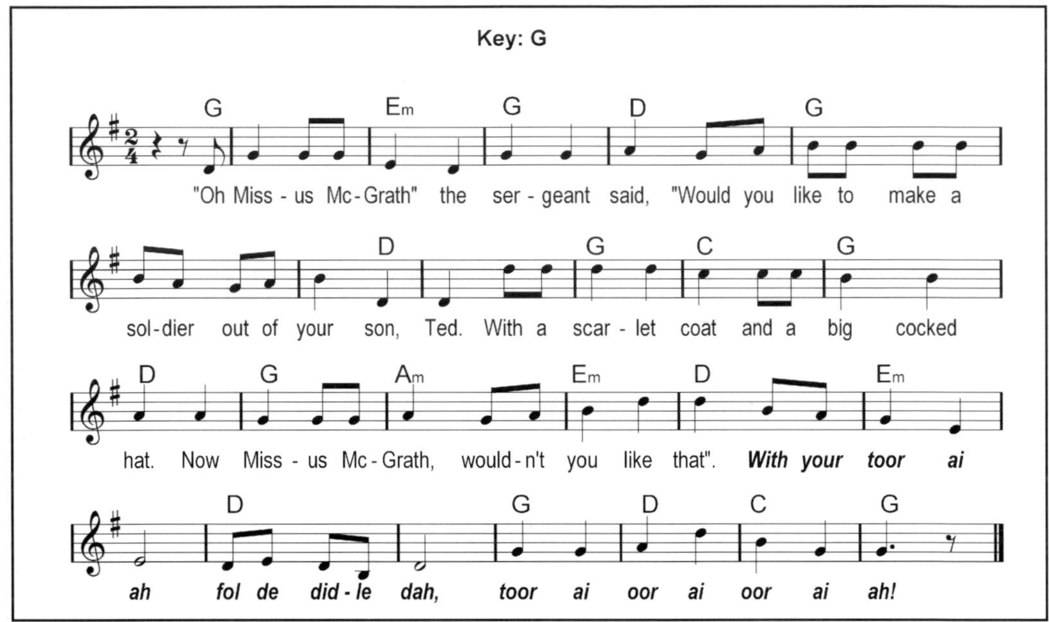

So Mrs McGrath lived on the sea shore, for the space of seven long years or more
Till she saw a ship sailing into the bay; "Here's my son Ted wisha clear the way". ***Chorus***

Oh Captain dear, where have you been, have you been a-sailing on the Mediterreen
Or have you any tidings of my son Ted, is the poor boy living or is he dead? ***Chorus***

Then up comes Ted without any legs, and in their place he has two wooden pegs
She kissed him a dozen times or two, saying "Holy Moses, 'tis isn't you" ***Chorus***

"Oh then were ye drunk or were ye blind, that ye left your two fine legs behind
Or was it walking upon the say*, wore yer two fine legs from the knees away?" ***Chorus***

"Oh I wasn't drunk and I wasn't blind, but I left my two fine legs behind
For a cannon ball on the fifth of May, took my two fine legs from my knees away" ***Chorus***

"Oh then Teddy me boy," the widow cried, "Yer two fine legs were yer mammy's pride
Them stumps of a tree won't do at all, why didn't ye run from the big cannon ball? ***Chorus***

All foreign wars I do proclaim, between Don John and the King of Spain
And by herrins I'll make them rue the time, that they swept the legs from a child of mine. ***Chorus***

Oh then if I had you back again, I'd never let ye go to fight the King of Spain
For I'd rather my Ted as he used to be, than the King of France and his whole Navy" ***Chorus***

*sea

(The melody of the second part of the chorus is a repeat of the first part)

This appears to be a satirical song, either poking fun at a certain anonymous individual, or at the IRA.
In any event, the person who wrote it kept very quiet about it!
In all of my research I can't find a single reference to either the subject matter, or the author.
I have come across quite a few versions of this ballad, each with minor variations.
References to Easter Monday (the 1916 Easter Rebellion) and the Black and Tans (see Additional Notes) suggests that it may have been written in the early 1920's, around the time of the War of Independence.
Mullingar is situated in the heart of Ireland in County Westmeath, about 51 miles from Dublin

Seven hundred Peelers couldn't catch him - catch him
The king sent out an order for to lash him - lash him
When Patrick came to Dublin town he stole an armoured car
And gave it to the I.R.A. brigade in Mullingar

On Easter Monday when the boys did hear the bugle's sound
Patrick raised the flag of war down in his native town
First he went to make his peace with dear old Father Maher
Then went and blew the barracks up, and wrecked half of Mullingar. ***Chorus***

When Ireland takes her place among the nations of the world
And her flag of orange white and green to the four winds is unfurled
When you read the roll of honour you will find marked with a star
Patrick Sarsfield Mulligan, the man from Mullingar! ***Chorus***

The Peeler And The Goat

This is am amusing ballad with nationalist anti-establishment overtones.
The melody is that of the old Irish air "An Buailteoir".
It was written by Diarmuid O'Riain, better known as Darby Ryan. He was born at Ashgrove, near the village of Bansha in County Tipperary, in 1777.
He was the youngest son of a wealthy farmer and was educated at the local hedge school. The attractions of his local area together with the political moods of the time afforded him much fodder for his poetry.
When Ryan heard reports of a local police patrol encountering a goat and impounding it he swiftly put pen to paper and wrote this satirical poem.
He died in 1855 and is buried in the old cemetary at Bansha. His headstone is rather unusual as it includes a prominent anchor. The story goes that the locals, commissioned to buy a headstone for Ryan, spent some of the funds for refreshments on the road. They were then forced to settle for a headstone commissioned for a local seafarer - hence the description - "Darby's Anchor".
The ballad became very popular throughout Ireland and was used as a taunt against the forces of Law.
The popularity of the song inspired others in a similar vein. "The Peeler and the Sow" set in County Clare, and "The Dog's Victory on the Peeler" set in County Kilkenny.
Sir Robert Peel was appointed Secretary of Ireland in 1812. One of his first acts was to establish a police force. The Irish people regarded this new force as another vehicle by which the Authorities could suppress them and deny them their liberty. The members of the new force were quickly labelled 'Peelers' and 'Bobbies' after their creator.
Bansha is situated between Cahir and Tipperary Town.
Cashel is also a town in Tipperary.
'Croppy' was the nickname given to insurgents fighting in the 1798 Rebellion.
'Ribbonmen' were members of a secret oath-bound society established for the protection of Catholics and the harrassment of Protestants, particularly strong in the northern parts of Ireland.
The Penal Laws were discriminatory laws against Catholics, passed by the Irish Parliament following the Battle of Aughrim in 1691.

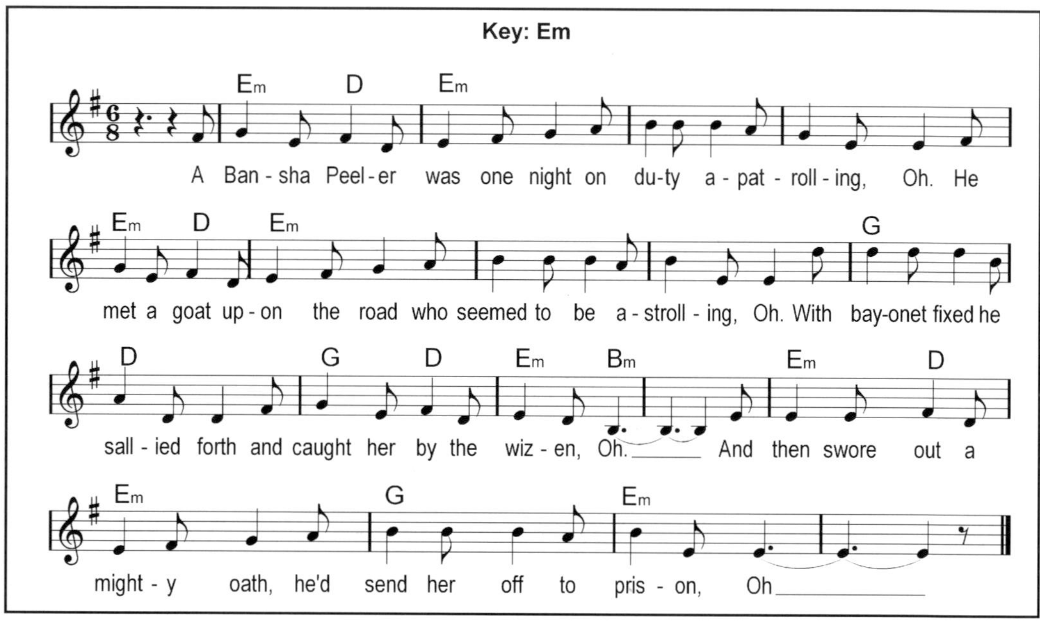

"Oh mercy, sirs," the goat replied: "Pray, let me tell my story, Oh
I am no rogue or Ribbonman, no Croppy, Whig or Tory, Oh
I'm guilty not of any crime of petty or high treason, Oh
And I'm sadly wanted at this time, for 'tis the milking season, Oh"

"It is in vain you do complain, or give your tongue such bridle, Oh
You're absent from your dwelling place, disorderly and idle, Oh
Your hoary locks will not avail, nor your sublime oration, Oh
For Grattan's Act will you transport, by your own information, Oh"

"This parish and this neighbourhood are peaceful, quiet, and tranquil, Oh
There's no disturbance here, thank God, and may it long continue so.
Your oath I don't regard a pin, to sign for my committal, Oh
My jury will be gentlemen, to grant me an acquittal, Oh"

"I'll soon chastise your impudence and insolvent behaviour, Oh
Well bound for Cashel you'll be sent, where you will find no favour, Oh
Impartial Billy Purefoy will sign your condemnation, Oh
And from there to Cork you'll be sent for speedy transportation, Oh"

"The Penal Laws I ne'er transgressed, by need or combination, Oh
I have no fixed place of abode, nor certain habitation, Oh
Bansha is my dwelling-place, where I was bred and born, Oh
Descended from an honest race, therefore your threats I scorn, Oh"

"Let the consequence be what it will, a peeler's power I'll let you know
I'll fetter you at all events and march you off to prison, Oh
You villain, sure you can't deny before a judge and jury, Oh
That I on you did find two spears which threatened me with fury, Oh"

"I'm certain if you were not drunk with whiskey, rum or brandy, Oh
You would not have such gallant spunk, or be so bold or manly, Oh
You readily would let me pass if I'd the sterling handy, Oh
To treat you to a poteen glass - O, 'tis then I'd be a dandy, Oh"

Come fill us up a flowing bowl, we'll drink a grand libation, Oh,
And toast a health to each true son throughout this grand old nation, Oh
We'll toast brave Ireland three times three, with pride and acclamation, Oh
May all her people be made free by speedy separation, Oh

GLASNEVIN CEMETERY, DUBLIN
The grave of Charles Stewart Parnell. See page 4

The Kerry Recruit

(The melody of the chorus is similar to the last two lines of the verse)

This was a popular anti-recruitment song similar in sentiment to "Johnny, I Hardly Knew Ye" (page 32) and "Mrs. McGrath" (page 34).
In this ballad the poor unfortunate subject was induced to 'take the king's shilling' and join the British Army. He was sent off to fight in the Crimean War, losing a leg in the process.

The Crimean War took place between 1854 and 1856 and it involved Britain and France as allies against Russia.
In those days you could find yourself on the wrong end of a six month jail sentence for singing anti-recruitment songs like this one!
Tralee is the County Capital of County Kerry, in the south of Ireland.

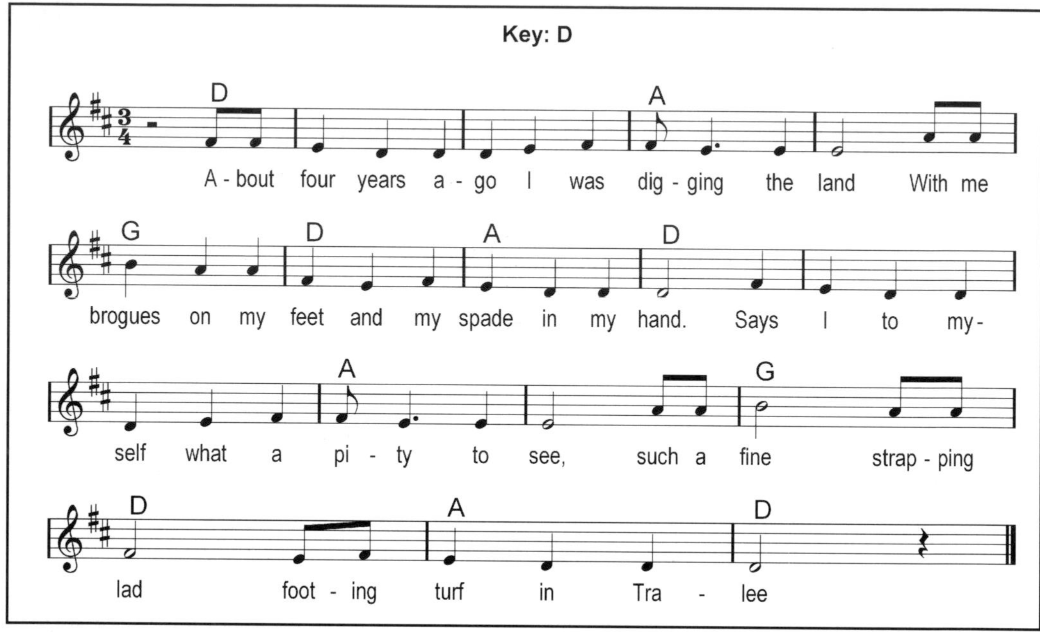

With me too-rem-a-nay - me too-rem-a-nay
Me too-rem-en-urem, en-urem a-nay.

So I buttoned my brogues and shook hands with my spade
And I took to the road like a dashing young blade
I met with the sergeant, he asked me to list
"Arrah, Sergeant" I said, "stick a bob in my fist". ***Chorus***

The first thing they gave me it was a red coat
With a wide strap of leather to tie around my throat
They gave me a quare thing; I asked what was that
And they told me it was a cockade for my hat. ***Chorus***

Oh the next thing they gave me it was a big gun
With powder and shot and a place for my thumb
Well, first she spit fire, boys, and then she spit smoke
And she gave a great leap and my shoulder near broke. ***Chorus***

The next place they sent me was down to the quay
On board a big warship bound for the Crimea
Three sticks in the middle all rolled round with sheet
And she walked on the water without any feet. ***Chorus***

When at the Crimea we landed quite sound
All cold, wet and hungry we lay on the ground
Next morning the bugle for action did call
And we got a hot breakfast of powder and ball. ***Chorus***

We fought at the Alma, likewise Inkerman,
But the Russians they whaled us at the Redan
When scaling a wall sure myself lost an eye
And a big Russian bullet ran away with my thigh. ***Chorus***

As there I lay bleeding upon the cold ground
Heads, arms and legs were scattered all round
Says I "If my ma and my brothers were nigh
They'd bury me decent and raise a loud cry". ***Chorus***

They fetched me a doctor and soon staunched my blood
And they made me an elegant leg made of wood
They gave me a pension of ten pence a day
Contented with Sheila I'd live on half pay. ***Chorus***

General Post Office, O'Connell Street, Dublin
Headquarters of the Provisional Government
and the insurgents during the 1916 Rebellion

The Scarriff Martyrs

This ballad concerns an incident which occurred during the War of Independence (1919 - 1921).

The War of Independence was the campaign waged by the Irish Volunteers and the Irish Republican Army against the British authorities in Ireland which culminated in the signing of the Anglo-Irish Treaty and ultimately to the formation of the Irish Republic.

The Irish rebels, under Michael Collins, engaged in a highly effective form of guerrilla warfare to gradually break down the effectiveness of the British occupying forces and the Royal Irish Constabulary. In response to this the British administration deployed regular troops together with a newly created force known as the 'Black and Tans" (see Additional Notes).

In mid-November 1920 the Black and Tans arrested four Volunteers, Alfie Rogers, Michael Egan, Michael 'Brod' McMahon and Martin Gildea. They were taken to the bridge of Killaloe, which separates Counties Clare and Tipperary, and shot dead. The British authorities said that they were shot trying to escape but local witnesses hotly refuted this.

The four men became known as 'The Scarriff Martyrs' (Scarriff being a small town nearby to Killaloe)

The killings took place on November 16th 1920 and between 15 and 20 shots were fired at the unarmed men.

Annually in or around November 15th a wreath in memory of the four Scarriff Martyrs is placed at the monument on the bridge of Killaloe.

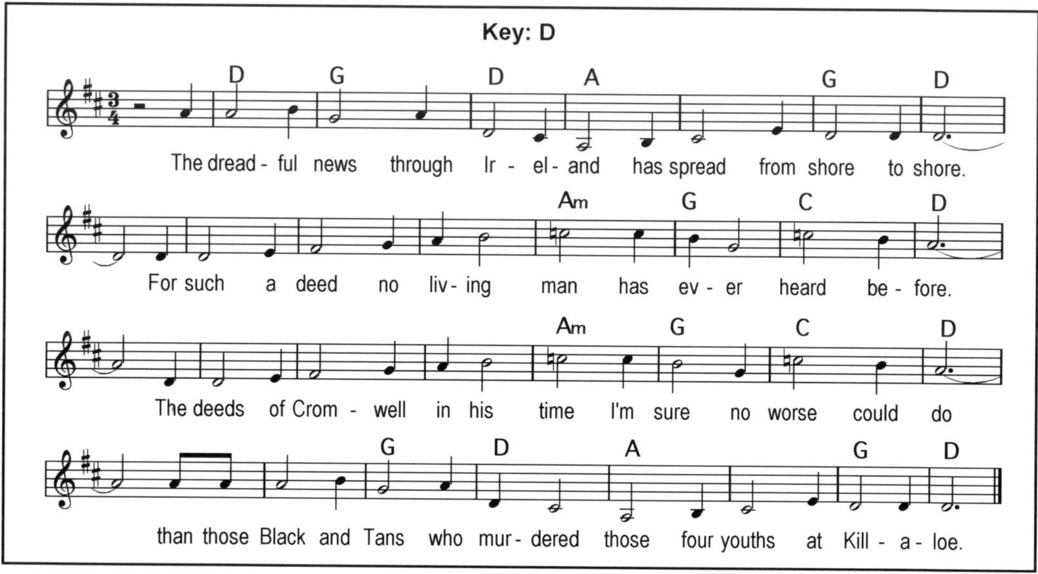

Three of the four were on the run and searched for all around
Until with this brave Egan lad from Williamstown was found
They asked him were the boys inside; in honour he proved true
Because he would not tell the pass he was shot in Killaloe.

On the fourth day of November, that day of sad renown
They were sold and traced through Galway to that house in Williamstown
They never got a fighting chance but were captured while asleep
And the way that they ill-treated them would cause your blood to creep.

They bound them tight both hands and feet with twine they could not break
And they brought them down to Killaloe by steamer on the lake
Without clergy, judge or jury upon the bridge they shot them down
And their blood flowed with the Shannon, convenient to the town.

With three days of perseverance, their bodies they let go
At ten o'clock at night their funeral passed through Ogonolloe
They were kept in Scarriff chapel for two nights and a day
Now in that place of rest they lie; kind people for them pray.

If you were at their funeral, it was an awful sight
To see the local clergy and they all dressed up in white
Such a sight as these four martyrs in one grave was never seen
For they died to save the flag they loved, the orange white and green.

Now that they are dead and gone I hope in peace they'll rest
Like all their Irish brave comrades, forever among the blessed
The day will come when all will know who sold the lives away
Of young McMahon, Rogers, valiant Egan and Gildea.

KILLALOE, CLARE
The bridge over Lough Derg where the Scarriff Martyrs were shot down

Skibbereen

This is a ballad about emigration and eviction.
The Great Famine occurred in Ireland between 1845 and 1849. At that time the standard staple diet of the Irish peasant was potatoes, potatoes, and more potatoes. Millions of Irish people died when the potato crops were ravaged with potato blight (Phytophthora infestans) over successive years. Those who could afford it boarded the notorious 'coffin ships' and the lucky ones who survived the journey started new lives in North America.
Small tenant farmers suffered eviction if they defaulted on the rent payment to their landlords, mostly English gentlemen who lived in London and employed ruthless Agents to look after their interests in Ireland. The eviction process did not take the form of merely forcibly removing the tenant farmer and his family from the cottage. It was standard for the Agent to arrive at the tenant's cottage with the Eviction Order in the company of the local Sheriff and a handful of local constabulary. The front door would be battered down, the family's belongings removed and thrown on the ground outside, and the cottage would often be burned to the ground or severely damaged. The Irish Constabulary recorded 117,000 evictions, affecting approximately 587,000 people, between 1846 and 1887. If you also take into account the 'voluntary surrenders', the number of displaced Irish peasants during that period would be considerably higher.
Skibbereen is a market town situated in West Cork in the south west of Ireland. Some of the most stunning scenery in Ireland is to be found in West Cork, along the winding roads which join the towns of Schull, Skibbereen, Ross Carbery and Clonakilty. Skibbereen is situated in what was once a very poor and somewhat bleak region. It is one of the areas that suffered most during the Great Famine.
You can hear Michael Collins (Liam Neeson) reciting a verse of this ballad while in Kitty Kiernan's house, in the film "Michael Collins".

Oh son, I loved my native land with energy and pride
Until a blight came o'er my crops; my sheep and cattle died
My rent and taxes were so high I could not them redeem
And that's the cruel reason why I left old Skibbereen.

It is so well I do recall that bleak December day
The landlord and the sheriff came to drive us all away
They set my roof on fire with their cursed English spleen
And that's another reason why I left old Skibbereen.

Your mother too, God rest her soul, fell on the snowy ground
Her treasured life's possessions they lay trampled all around
She never rose but passed away, from life to mortal dream
And found a quiet resting place in dear old Skibbereen.

And you were only two years old and feeble was your frame
I could not leave you with my friends; you bore your father's name
I wrapped you in a blanket at the dead of night unseen
I heaved a sigh and bade goodbye to dear old Skibbereen.

Oh father dear the day will come when vengeance loud will call
All Irishmen with stern of faith will rally one and all
I'll be the man to lead the van beneath the flag of green
And loud and high we'll raise the cry "Remember Skibbereen!"

25 Northumberland Road, Dublin
It was in this house, and three other buildings nearby, that seventeen members of the Irish Volunteers "C" Company under the command of Lieutenant Michael Malone engaged with an entire battalion of British Army 'Sherwood Foresters' and kept them at bay for over five hours in the 1916 Rising. The 'Sherwood Foresters' suffered very heavy casualties before eventually storming the buildings. Lieutenant Malone was killed in action.

The Wild Colonial Boy

The hero of this ballad may be based on an outlaw called Jack Donahue who was a criminal transported to Australia in the early 1800's. He escaped from captivity in Australia and resumed his life of crime. He was captured and shot in 1830.

This ballad is very well known and sung throughout Ireland though the origins of the song itself are unclear. Like most old ballads there are many versions to be found. One version has the Wild Colonial Boy as 'Jack Doolan'; another as 'Jack Donahue'. Apparently there is an Australian Bush Ballad entitled 'Bold Jack Donahue' with some lines similar to the Wild Colonial Boy. There is a town in Australia called Beechwood, situated on the main road between Melbourne and Sydney, which was a major gold mining town in the last century and a Judge presided there by the name of McEvoy. So there is some truth in the ballad. But the name of the 'Wild Colonial Boy'? Who knows!

Castlemaine is a small picturesque village in County Kerry, situated on the south east coast of Ireland; but it is also a small town in Australia with a history of goldmining.

This is another example of a ballad which praises the exploits of the highwayman, or 'rapparee' as they were called in Ireland. See "Brennan on the Moor" - page 30.

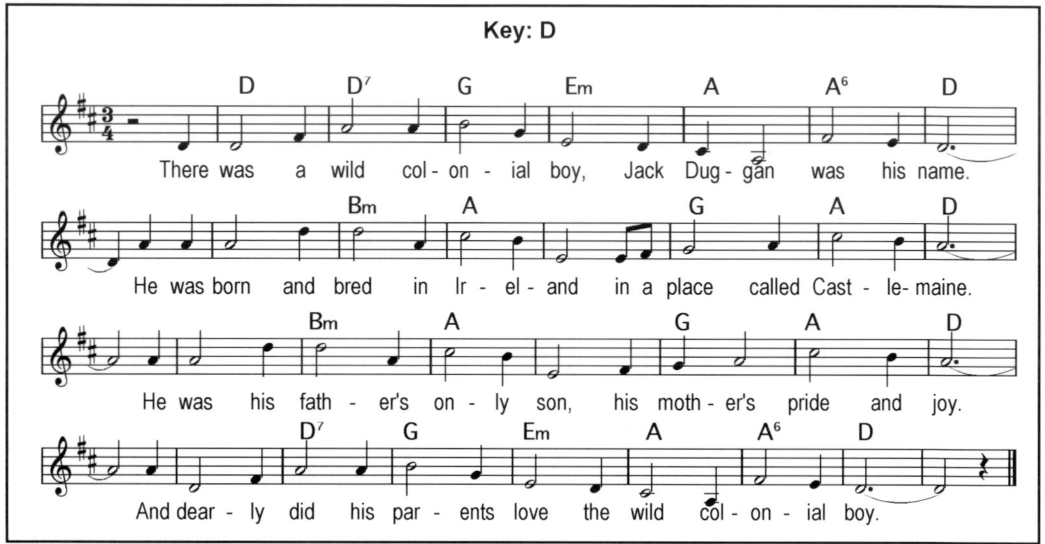

At the early age of sixteen years he left his native home
And to Australia's sunny shores he was inclined to roam
He helped the poor he robbed the rich, their crops he would destroy
A terror to Australia was the Wild Colonial Boy.

For two long years this daring youth ran on his wild career
With a heart that knew no danger and a soul that felt no fear
He held the Beechwood coach up and he robbed Judge McEvoy
Who, trembling, gave his gold up to the Wild Colonial Boy.

He bade the Judge "Good Morning" and he told him to beware
For he never robbed an honest judge who acted 'on the square'
"Yet you would rob a mother of her only pride and joy
And breed a race of outlaws like the Wild Colonial Boy".

One morning on the prairie while Jack Duggan rode along
While listening to the mocking bird a-singing out his song
Out jumped three troopers fierce and grim, Kelly, Davis and Fitzroy
Were detailed for to capture him, the Wild Colonial Boy.

"Surrender now Jack Duggan, you can see we're three to one
Surrender in our Queen's name for you are a plund'ring son"
Jack drew two pistols from his belt and glared upon Fitzroy
"I'll fight but not surrender!" cried the Wild Colonial Boy.

He fired a shot at Kelly and he brought him to the ground
He fired a shot at Davis too, who fell dead at the sound
But a bullet pierced his brave young heart from the pistol of Fitzroy
And that was how they captured him, the Wild Colonial Boy.

Jack Duggan's Bar, Castlemaine, Kerry

The Boys Of Mullaghbawn

This is a mournful Northern Ireland ballad about transportation.
Mullaghbawn is a small village in South Armagh, Northern Ireland.
In the 18th century Mullaghbawn was part of the Forkhill Estate, owned by a benevolant landlord, Richard Jackson ('Squire Jackson'). Jackson was very popular among his tenants. He lived on the estate, worked the land and encouraged his tenants to do likewise. He died in 1787.
Jackson's successor - probably the 'vile deceiving stranger' in the song - was much less popular.
There is no detail in the song about the transgressions of the Boys, but it could relate to membership of the United Irishmen, or to the commission of some agrarian offence.
There are also hints that the Boys had attempted to abduct a local 'noble lady', a practice which was common enough in the late 18th century.
'The Cuckoo' is the name of the ship in which they were transported.
The Irish singer, Christy Moore, sings a wonderful lamenting version of this ballad on his album, "Christy Moore" (1976).

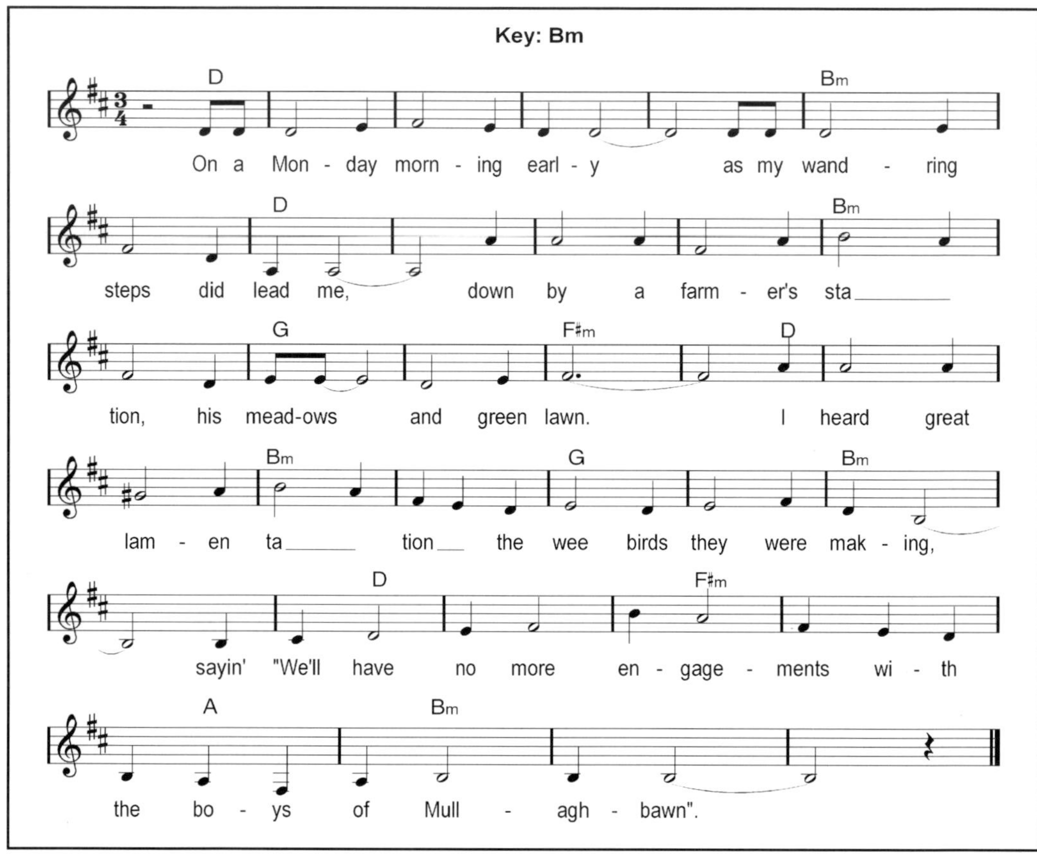

I beg your pardon ladies and ask you this one favour
I hope it is no treason, on you I now must call
I'm weeping late and early, my heart is nigh to breaking
All for a noble lady that lives near Mullaghbawn

Squire Jackson he's unequalled for honour and for reason
He never turned a traitor or betrayed the Rights Of Man
But now we are in danger from a vile deceiving stranger
Who has ordered transportation for the boys of Mullaghbawn

And as they crossed the ocean, I'm told the ship in motion
Would stand in wild commotion as if the seas ran dry
The trout and salmon gaping as 'The Cuckoo' left her station
Saying "Fare you well old Erin, and the hills of Mullaghbawn"

To end my lamentation we're all in consternation
None cares for recreation until the day do dawn
For without hesitation we're charged with combination
And sent for transportation from the hills of Mullaghbawn

Dublin Castle Upper Yard
The headquarters of English and British
administration in Ireland for over 800 years

Dunlavin Green

This song narrates and condemns one of the many atrocities committed by the Loyalists during the 1798 Rebellion. Thirty-six Yeomen who were suspected United Irish sympathisers were imprisoned in the town of Dunlavin, Wicklow. On 26th May 1798, without reason or provocation an English officer, Captain William Ryves of the Dunlavin Cavalry, led them out to the village green and summarily executed them. (The ballad erroneously attributes the blame to Captain Morley Saunders of the Saundersgrove infantry.)

A detailed account of the incident can be found in Fitzpatrick's "The Sham Squire and the informers of 1798"

'Dwyer' refers to Michael Dwyer (1771-1826), leader of a small band of 1798 insurgents who took to the Wicklow hills following the failure of the 1798 Rebellion.

For further information on the 1798 Insurrection and Yeomanry see the Additional Notes.

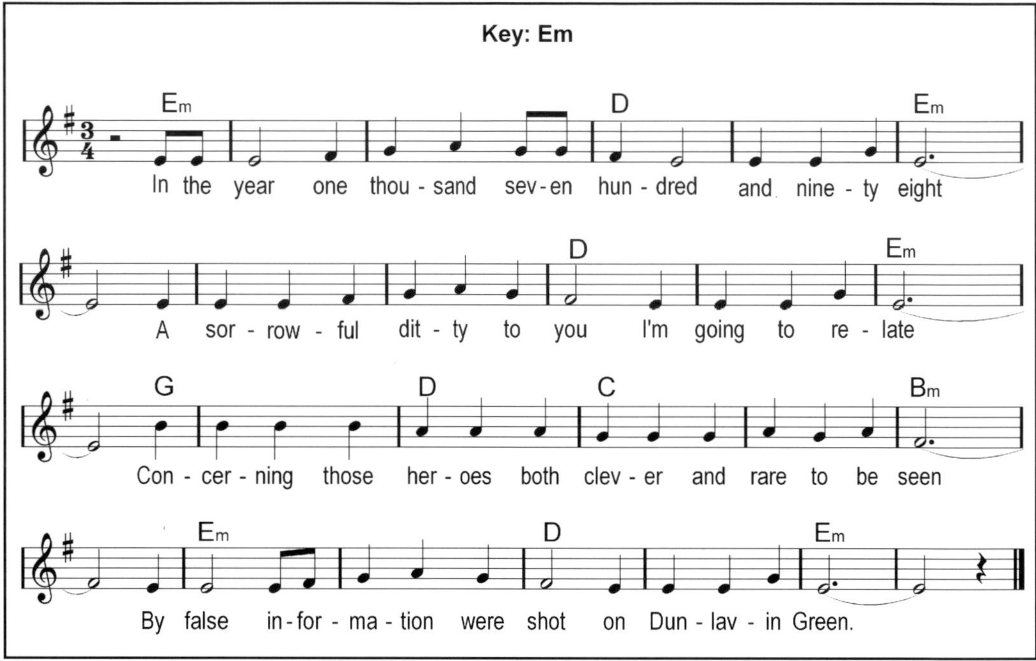

Woe to you, Saunders; disgrace me you never shall
That the tears of the widows may melt you like snow before the sun
Those fatherless orphans! their cries nor moans can't be screened
For the loss of their fathers, who were shot upon Dunlavin Green

Quite easy they led us as prisoners through the town
Like lambs to the slaughter on the plain we were forced to kneel down
Such sorrow and terror were never before there seen
To see the blood run in streams down the dykes of Dunlavin Green

Some of our heroes are 'listed and gone far away
There are some of them dead, and some of them crossing the sea
As for poor Andy Ryan, his mother distracted has been
For the loss of her son, who was shot upon Dunlavin Green

As for Andy Farrell, I'm sure he has cause to complain
And likewise the two Duffys, I'm sure they may well do the same
Dwyer on the mountain to the Orange he owes a great spleen
For the loss of his comrades, who were shot upon Dunlavin Green

That we may live happy the joyful tidings to hear
When we will have satisfaction for the murders they did that year
There were thirty-six heroes, both clever and rare to be seen
Both loyal and united, shot one day on Dunlavin Green

Now to conclude and finish my mournful tale
I hope all good Christians to pray for their souls will not fail
Their souls in white pigeons a-flying to heaven were seen
On the very same day they were shot upon Dunlavin Green

Dunlavin Green

The Enniskillen Dragoon

This ballad was written by George Sigerson (1836 - 1925) who was born near Strabane in County Tyrone (Northern Ireland). Sigerson took a degree in medicine in 1859. He taught himself Irish and took honours and a prize at a special Celtic examination in his final year in medical school.
He married and settled in Dublin. He was Professor of Botany and later of Zoology at the Catholic University Medical School and The National University of Ireland.
He wrote and edited many books, including "The Poets And Poetry Of Munster" (1860), and "Bards Of The Gael And Gall" (1897). He lived at No. 3 Clare Street in Dublin city centre and his home was a refuge and gathering-place for all those interested in Irish music and literature. He was one of the first members of the Irish Free State Seanad (Senate).
In 1911 George Sigerson inaugurated The Sigerson Cup, a trophy for a Gaelic Football Championship among Higher Level Institutions, and the Cup has been played for ever since. The Sigerson Cup is widely regarded as a breeding ground for future inter-county football players.
Dragoons originally were mounted infantrymen armed with fire-spitting muskets.

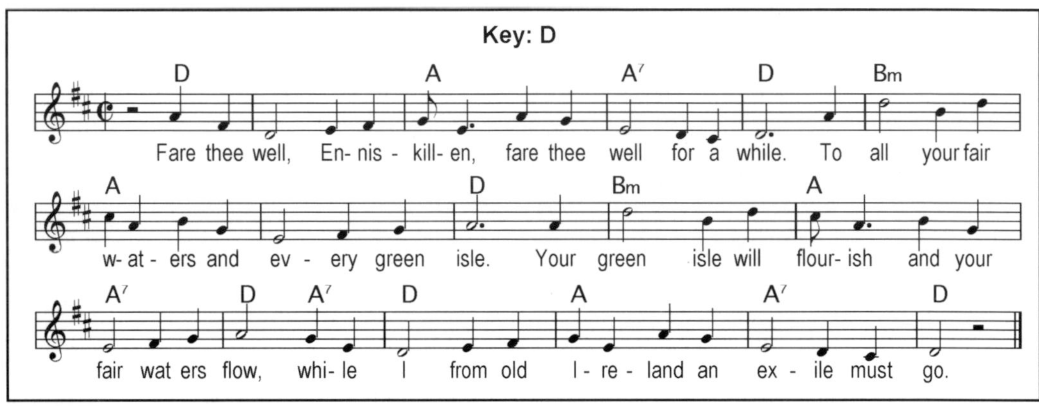

Oh they were all dressed out just like gentlemen's' sons
With their bright shining swords and new carbine guns
With their silver mounted pistols she observed them full soon
All because that she loved her Enniskillen Dragoon.

The bright sons of Mars as they stood to the right
Their armour did shine like the bright stars at night
She says "Lovely Willie, you've enlisted too soon
To serve as a Royal Enniskillen Dragoon".

"Oh beautiful Flora your pardon I crave
From now and forever I will act as your slave
Your parents insult you both morning and noon
For fear you should wed your Enniskillen Dragoon".

"Oh now, dearest Willie you should mind what you say
Until I'm of age my parents I must obey
But when you're leaving Ireland they will surely change their tune
Saying 'The Lord be he with you Enniskillen Dragoon' ".

Farewell Enniskillen fare thee well for a while
And all around the borders of Erin's green isle
And when the wars are over I'll return in full bloom
And they'll all welcome home their Enniskillen Dragoon.

Now the war is over they've returned home at last
The regiment's in Dublin and Willie got a pass
Last Sunday they were married and bold Willie was the groom
And now she enjoys her Enniskillen Dragoon.

TREATY STONE, LIMERICK CITY
It was on this stone that the Treaty of Limerick was signed between the Jacobites and Williamites in 1691, following the seige of the city. Under the terms of the Treaty Patrick Sarsfield, Jacobite General, was permitted to leave Ireland for France with his force of 10,000 troops - the first movement of what became known as 'The Flight of the Wild Geese'.

Follow Me Up To Carlow

This is a rousing and gory ballad, reputed to have been written by Patrick J. McCall (1861 - 1919). The ballad celebrates the victory of Fiach McHugh O'Byrne (c. 1544 - 1597) over the English forces at Glenmalure in 1580.

Fiach McHugh O'Byrne was the leader of the O'Byrne clan in Co. Wicklow and was a major thorn in England's side.

In 1580 the newly arrived Lord Deputy Leonard Grey decided to confront O'Byrne and his ally, Viscount Baltinglass. Grey sent half of his army under the leadership of one George Moore into County Wicklow to sort out the problem. On August 25th 1580 in a battle known as "The Baltinglass Revolt' O'Byrne defeated the English troops at Glenmalure in County Wicklow (south of Dublin), killing at least 30 of them including Moore himself. He later burned the southern outskirts of Dublin.

O'Byrne was relentlessly pursued by the English who eventually killed him on May 8th 1597. His head was displayed on the battlements of Dublin Castle.

"Black Fitzwilliam" refers to Sir William Fitzwilliam (1526 - 1599), the most experienced Elizabethan administrator in Ireland and reputedly the most corrupt. He presided for a time as Chief Governor of Ireland.

Glen Imaal, Clonmore and Tassagart are towns and townlands which were part of O'Byrne's territories. The "English Pale" was the term used for the region surrounding Dublin on the east coast of Ireland which was a fortified area of English rule in the 16th century. It comprised mainly of the counties of Dublin, Meath, Kildare and Louth.

Carlow is the second smallest county in Ireland (350 square miles) and is adjacent to County Wicklow.

My mother's maiden name is O'Byrne and all of her family come from County Wicklow near the Wicklow/Carlow border. Which means that I'm probably related in some way or other to Fiach McHugh O'Byrne!

See the swords at Glen Imaal, a-flashing o'er the English Pale
See all the children of the Gael beneath O'Byrne's banners
Rooster of a fighting stock, would you let a Saxon cock
Crow out upon an Irish rock; rise up and teach him manners. ***Chorus***

From Tassagart to Clonmore there flows a stream of Saxon gore
And great is Rory Og O'More at sending the loons to Hades
White is sick, Grey has fled; now for Black Fitzwilliam's head
We'll send it over, dripping red, to Queen Liza and her ladies. ***Chorus***

The Valley of Glenmalure, Wicklow
The remote and inaccessible Glenmalure Valley.
A memorial stone commemorates the Battle of Glenmalure, 1580.

The Wearing Of The Green

There are many versions of this ballad to be found. This version is probably the best known. It was written by Dion Boucicault (1822 - 1890) and included in his play "Arrah-na-Pogue" which was first performed in Dublin in 1865.

Boucicault was born in Dublin, the son of a French refugee and Irish mother. He was a popular playwright in London before the age of twenty. From 1853 to 1869 he moved to the U.S.A. and was equally successful there. He returned to Britain where he died in 1890. Some of his most celebrated works include "The Colleen Bawn", "The Octoroon" and "The Shaugraun".

This is very much a patriotic ballad which laments the suppression by the English administration in Ireland of all Nationalist symbols and sentiment. During the 18th century the colour green became more and more symbolic of Ireland's struggle for freedom. This may be on account of its affiliation to the shamrock, the humble three-leaf plant that had already become a religious emblem and a badge of nationality by 1700. The Cork Volunteers in the 1770's used to sing a song entitled "The Shamrock Cockades". The colour rapidly acquired a political meaning.

The patriot delegates wore green ribands across their shoulders while marching in procession to a convention in Dublin in November 1783. Green handkerchiefs and scarves were waved from the windows as they passed by. When the United Irishmen adopted green as their symbol for a free Ireland the colour was regarded as seditious by the English authorities. In an edition of "The Press" of November 25th 1797 it was written that a green ribbon or handkerchief, even accidentally worn, being regarded as 'an emblem of affection to Ireland' would 'subject a man to imprisonment, transportation, the rope or the bayonet, and expose women to the brutal insults of the common soldiery'.

"Napper Tandy" refers to James Napper Tandy (c. 1737 - 1803), prominent member of the United Irishmen who was involved in the 1798 Rebellion. He was captured in Hamburg, returned to Ireland and sentenced to death but was deported to France in 1803.

This song has, broadly, the same air as "The Rising of the Moon" (page 20).

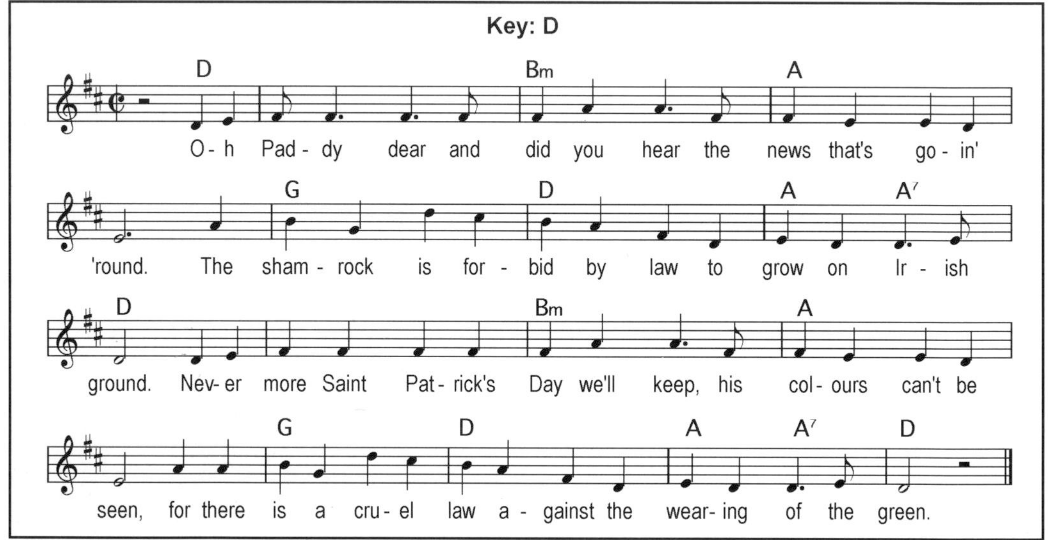

I met with Napper Tandy and he took me by the hand
He said "How's poor old Ireland; please tell how does she stand"
"She is the most distressful land that ever yet was seen
For they're hanging men and women for the wearing of the Green".

And if the colour we must wear is England's cruel red
Let it remind us of the blood that Ireland's sons have shed
Then take the shamrock from your hat and cast it on the sod
And never fear, 'twill take root there though under foot 'tis trod.

When laws can stop the blades of grass from growing where they grow
And when the leaves in summertime their colours dare not show
Then I will change the colour that I wear in my cáibin*
But 'til that day please God I stay a-wearing of the Green.

But if sometime the colour should be torn from Ireland's heart
Her sons with shame and sorrow from our shores will surely part
I've heard a whisper of a land that lies beyond the sea
Where rich and poor stand equal in the light of liberty.

So Erin we must leave you now; cast out by tyrant's hand
We'll treasure mother's blessing from a strange and distant land
Where England's cruel and viscous hand is never to be seen
And where, please God, we'll plough the sod, a-wearing of the Green.
*Pronounced "cawbeen" (cloth cap)

Scoil Éanna (St. Enda's School), Rathfarnham, Dublin
Where Padraig Pearse taught his pupils and planned the 1916 Rebellion. It is now a museum

Sean South From Garryowen

From about 1956 to 1963 the Irish Republican Army in the Republic of Ireland waged a 'border campaign' on police barracks and Custom Posts around the borders between Northern Ireland and the Republic.

This song is an Irish patriotic ballad commemorating a failed attack on a Royal Ulster Constabulary barracks in Brookborough, County Fermanagh on New Year's Eve 1957. The small band of men, members of the Patrick Pearse Column of the I.R.A., were led by Sean South who as the ballad says came from Garryowen, a district of Limerick city.

The raid went disastrously wrong and Sean South along with Feargal O'Hanlon from County Monaghan were killed in the ensuing skirmish.

Sean South's funeral was held on January 5th 1958 and the massive cortege included public representative and members of the Irish Government. He was buried in the Republican Plot in Mount St. Laurence Cemetary, Limerick.

Dublin, Cork, Fermanagh, Tyrone and Limerick are all counties in Ireland.

The reference to "Shannon" is the River Shannon, the largest river in Ireland. It flows out to the sea through Limerick city.

"Plunkett" is Joseph Plunkett (1887 - 1916), one of the leaders of the 1916 Rising and a signatory of the Irish Proclamation.

"Pearse" is Padraig Pearse (1879 - 1916), the leader of the 1916 Rising and also a signatory of the Irish Proclamation.

"Tone" is Theobald Wolfe Tone (1763 - 1798), one of the leaders of the 1798 Rebellion.

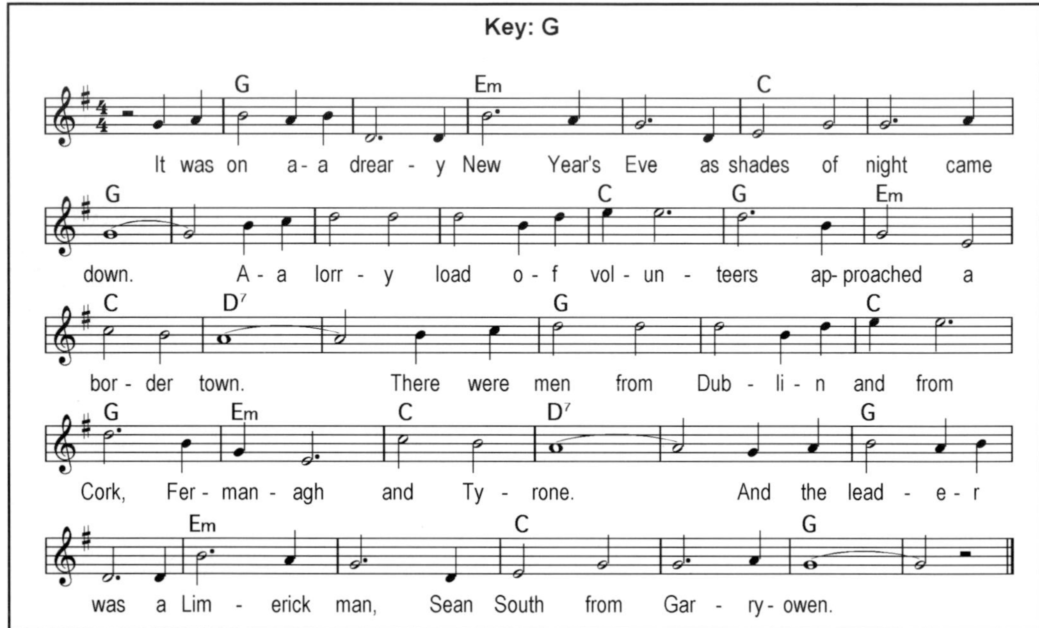

And as they moved along the street up to the barracks door
They scorned the dangers they would meet; the fate that lay in store
They were fighting for old Ireland's cause to claim their very own
And their leader was a Limerick man, Sean South from Garryowen.

But the sergeant spied their daring plan, he spied them through the door
With their sten guns and their rifle shots a hail of death did roar
And when that awful night had passed two men lay cold as stone
And one was from a border town and one from Garryowen.

No more he'll hear the seagulls cry o'er the murmuring Shannon tide
For he fell beneath a northern sky, brave Hanlon by his side
He has gone to join that gallant band of Plunkett, Pearse and Tone
Another martyr for old Ireland, Sean South from Garryowen.

The Boys Of Fairhill

A very popular ballad in Cork city and almost as well known as "The Banks" (page 22). Fairhill is a suburb of north Cork and this ballad is in praise of the local hurling team.
Hurling is one of our two most popular national games in Ireland (Gaelic Football being the other). There is a great devotion to hurling in Cork and there have been many fine Cork hurling teams victorious in the All Ireland Hurling Championships.
"Crubeens" are boiled pig's feet, a very popular dish in Cork. Patrick's Bridge is the main bridge over the River Lee which flows through Cork city and there is a statue of Father Matthew located beside the bridge. Father Matthew, known as the Apostle of Temperance, dedicated most of his life to persuading Irishmen to give up 'the demon drink'.

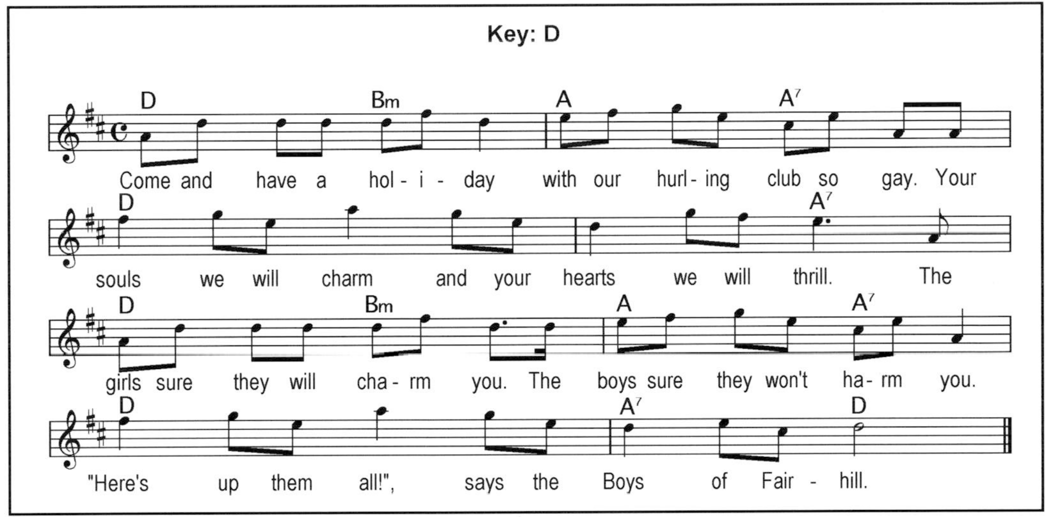

We'll go down by Sunday's Well, what might happen, who can tell
Heads, they might roll or some blood it might spill
We'll come back by Blackpool way when we've overcome the fray
"Here's up them all!" says thc Boys of Fairhill.

Jimmy Barry hooks the ball, we'll hook Jimmy, ball and all
"Here's up them all!" says the Boys of Fairhill
The Rockies thought they were the stars till they met the Saint Finbarr's
"Here's up them all!" says the Boys of Fairhill.

Kathy Barry sells crubeens, fairly bursting at the seams
Sure for to cure and more sure for to kill
The stench on Patrick's Bridge is wicked, how does Father Matthew stick it
"Here's up them all!" says the Boys of Fairhill.

VINEGAR HILL, WEXFORD
The ruined windmill on the summit of Vinegar Hill which served as a fort for the insurgents at the climax of the 1798 Rebellion in Wexford. The defeat of the insurgents was at the Battle of Vinegar Hill on June 21st 1798

Slievenamon

This ballad is recognised by Tipperary folk throughout the world as their County Anthem and can be heard loud and clear at all major 'Tipp' occasions, particularly Hurling and Gaelic Football matches.

It was written by Charles J. Kickham (1828 - 1882) and was originally known as "The Maid Of Slievenamon". Kickham came from Mullinahone in County Tipperary (situated in central Ireland) and was a member of a prosperous family. He was a journalist and nationalist and joined the Fenian movement in 1861.

Two years later he moved to Dublin and worked on the Fenian weekly newspaper 'The Irish People'. He was arrested and imprisoned in 1865 and released in 1869. By this time he was regarded as one of the leading nationalists in Ireland. In 1873 he was appointed President of the revolutionary Irish Republican Brotherhood (an organisation which evolved out of the failed 1867 Fenian Rising), a position he held until his death in 1882.

He was a noted ballad writer and also wrote a number of books, of which "Knocknagow" is his most famous.

The mountains of Slievenamon are located in the south-east of County Tipperary. The heatherlands, meadows and woods of Slievenamon cover an area of about 7,000 acres. The Slievenamon mountains rise to 2,370 feet at their highest point and dominate the surrounding plains.

There is another Irish ballad called "Sliabh Na mBan", a nationalist ballad about the plight of Ireland in her attempts to achieve independence.

Twas not the grace of her queenly air; nor her cheek of the rose's glow
Nor her soft dark eyes or her flowing hair; nor was it her lily-white brow
'Twas the soul of truth and of melting youth and a smile like the summer's dawn
That stole my heart away on that soft summer day in the valley near Slievenamon.

In the Festival Hall by the wave-washed shore, there my restless spirit cries
"My love, oh my love, shall I ne'er see you more and my land will you never uprise?"
By night and by day, I ever ever pray while so lonely my life flows on
But to see our flag unrolled and my true-love to enfold in the valley near Slievenamon.

Highland Paddy

This is a patriotic ballad made famous through recordings of it by many Irish folk and ballad groups.
Kilkenny city is a large town situated in central Ireland, with its civic and ecclesiastical roots deep in the past.
For further information about the Fenians see the Additional Notes

And in the morning we rose early, just before the break of dawn
Blackbirds singing in the bushes, greetings to a smiling morn
Gather 'round me men of Ireland, all ye Fenians gather round
Hand to hand with sword and musket, spill the blood upon this holy ground. ***Chorus***

There is a glen beside the river, just outside Kilkenny town
There we met this noble captain, men lay dying upon the ground
There is a grave down by the river, a mile outside Kilkenny town
There we laid our noble Captain, birds were silent when this Fenian died. ***Chorus***

For all my life I will remember, I'll remember night and day
That once I rode into Kilkenny and I heard the noble Captain say. ***Chorus***

Kelly From Killane

This ballad was written by P.J. McCall who also wrote "Boulavogue" (page 68).
The song honours John Kelly, one of the local heroes of the 1798 Rebellion in Wexford.
Kelly was the son of a Killane merchant and took part in the Battle of New Ross. He was under orders from Bagenal Harvey, the Wexford commander, to proceed with an army of 800 United Irishmen towards New Ross and to attack the English outposts but under no circumstances to attack the town itself. Harvey had worked out a detailed plan to take New Ross by simultaneously attacking through its three main gates. But on June 5th 1798, for reasons which are to this day unknown, Kelly's forces attacked New Ross through the 'Three Bullet Gate', successfully broke through, and continued on into the town itself. The ensuing disarray, confusion and lack of direction eventually led to the defeat of the rebel forces.
Kelly was wounded in Michael Street, New Ross and was recovering in Wexford Town when he was arrested by the English. He was subsequently hanged on Wexford Bridge.
'Shelmalier' is a townland of Wexford and the farmers there were accustomed to hunting wild fowl on the North Sloblands. Their 'long barrelled guns' proved to be very effective against the English forces during the rebellion. 'Forth' and 'Bargy' are also townlands in County Wexford.
For further information on the 1798 Rebellion see the Additional Notes.

"Tell me who is that giant with the gold curling hair; he who rides at the head of your band
Seven feet is his height with some inches to spare; and he looks like a king in command"
"Ah my lads, that's the pride of the bold Shelmaliers; 'mongst our greatest of heroes, a man
Fling your beavers aloft and give three ringing cheers; for John Kelly, the boy from Killane".

Enniscorthy's in flames and old Wexford is won; and the Barrow, tomorrow, we will cross
On a hill o'er the town we have planted a gun; that will batter the gateway of Ross
All the Forth men and Bargy men march o'er the heath; with brave Harvey to lead on the van
But the foremost of all in that grim gap of death; will be Kelly, the boy from Killane.

But the gold sun of freedom grew darkened at Ross; and it set by the Slaney's red waves
And poor Wexford, stripped naked, hung high on a cross; and her heart pierced by traitors and slaves
Glory O! Glory O! To her brave sons who died; for the cause of long downtrodden man
Glory O! To Mount Leinster's own darling and pride; dauntless Kelly, the boy from Killane.

'Three Bullet Gate', New Ross, Wexford
The remains of the 'Three Bullet Gate' which was stormed by John Kelly and his forces during the Battle of New Ross in 1798

A Nation Once Again

This ballad has been one of the main anthems of Irish revolutionary movements for the past 150 years.
Written by Thomas Davis (1814 - 1845), the ballad reflects the aspiration of the Young Ireland movement of the 1840's of which he was leader. Davis, the son of an English army surgeon, was born in County Cork. Educated at Trinity College in Dublin, he espoused many of his thoughts and ideas for Irish Nationhood in 'The Nation' a weekly newspaper which he founded in October 1842. He also sought to bring a sense of 'Irish Nationality' to the Irish people through the ballads published in 'The Nation', this being one of them. He also wrote another ballad in this book, "The West's Awake" (page 74).
Davis sought to introduce a new concept to the writing of Irish 'national' ballads. Prior to 'The Nation' most ballads were written as spontaneous and emotional reactions to events and circumstances as they occurred. Davis was determined to utilise the Irish ballad as an instrument to enable and encourage Irish people to reflect on the principle of Irish nationhood.
Davis died suddenly in September 1845 from an attack of scarlet fever at the age of 31 years.
For further information on Young Ireland and 'The Nation' see the Additional Notes.

And from that time through wildest woe that hope has shone a far light
Nor could love's brightest summer glow, outshine that solemn starlight
It seemed to watch above my head in forum field and fane
Its angel voice sang 'round my head, a nation once again. ***Chorus***

It whispered too that freedom's ark and service high and holy
Would be profaned by feelings dark and passions vain or lowly
For freedom comes from God's right hand and needs a godly train
And righteous men must make our land a nation once again. ***Chorus***

So as I grew from boy to man I bent me to that bidding
My spirit of each selfish plan and cruel passion ridding
For thus I hoped some day to aid; oh can such hope be vain
When my dear country can be made a nation once again. ***Chorus***

Statue of Thomas Davis
Situated in College Green, Dublin

(Verses and chorus have the same melody)

This is an old ballad popular throughout Ireland. The ballad seems to start in the middle of a story and there are obviously some verses before the first one here, but I have never come across them.

Singing mush mush mush toor-a-lie-addy; sing mush mush mush toor-a-lie-ay
There was ne'er a gassoon* in the village dared tread on the tail of me coat.

'Twas there I learned all of my courting; many lessons I took in the art
Till Cupid the blackguard, in sporting; an arrow drove straight through my heart
Molly Connor she lived right beside me; and tender lines to her I wrote
If you dare say one wrong word against her; I'll tread on the tail of your coat. ***Chorus***

But a blackguard called Mickey Moloney; he stole her affections away
He had money and I hadn't any; so I sent him a challenge next day
That evening we met at the woodbine; the Shannon we crossed in a boat
And I leathered him with my shillelagh; for he trod on the tail of my coat. ***Chorus***

My fame spread abroad through the nation; and folks came a-flocking to see
And they cried out without hesitation; "You're a fighting man, Billy McGee"
I cleaned out the Finnegan faction; and I licked all the Murphys afloat
If you're in for a row or a ruction just tread on the tail of me coat. ***Chorus***

* Young boy

Come To The Bower

This is a patriotic ballad, made famous by recordings by The Clancy Brothers and also The Dubliners.

It is a call to all Irishmen abroad to return to Ireland and take Ireland back from the English occupiers. Consequently there are many references in this ballad to great and heroic deeds of Irishmen in the past, designed to stir up the blood of all Irish people abroad.

"O'Neill" refers to Hugh O'Neill (1550 - 1616), Earl of Tyrone. "O'Donnell" refers to 'Red Hugh' O'Donnell (1572 - 1602) Lord of Tirconnell (see page 24). "Lord Lucan" refers to the patriot leader Patrick Sarsfield, Earl of Lucan (1655 - 1693). "O'Connell" refers to Daniel O'Connell (1775 - 1847) who secured Catholic emancipation from the Penal Laws and is know as 'The Liberator'. "Brian drove the Danes" refers to Brian Boru, High King of Ireland, whose army defeated the Danes at the Battle of Clontarf in 1014. "Benburb" refers to the Battle of Benburb which took place near the town of Benburb in County Tyrone in 1646, a battle between the Irish under Owen Roe O'Neill and the Scottish under General Munroe. 3000 Scottish troops were slain and the Irish losses amounted to only 40. It was an overwhelming victory for the Irish.

"Blackwater" refers to Blackwatertown in County Armagh, whose English garrison was successfully blockaded by Hugh O'Neill in 1598. "Dungannon" refers to the town of Dungannon, County Tyrone, site of the ancient fortress of the O'Neill clan.

New Ross, Wexford and Gorey are towns in County Wexford which saw scenes of fierce fighting and bloodshed during the 1798 Rebellion. (For further information about the 1798 Rebellion see the Additional Notes)

A 'bower' is a shady and hidden enclosure or recess in a garden, indicating that the singer of this ballad wants all Irishmen to meet with him in a secret location to plan the overthrow of the English forces in Ireland.

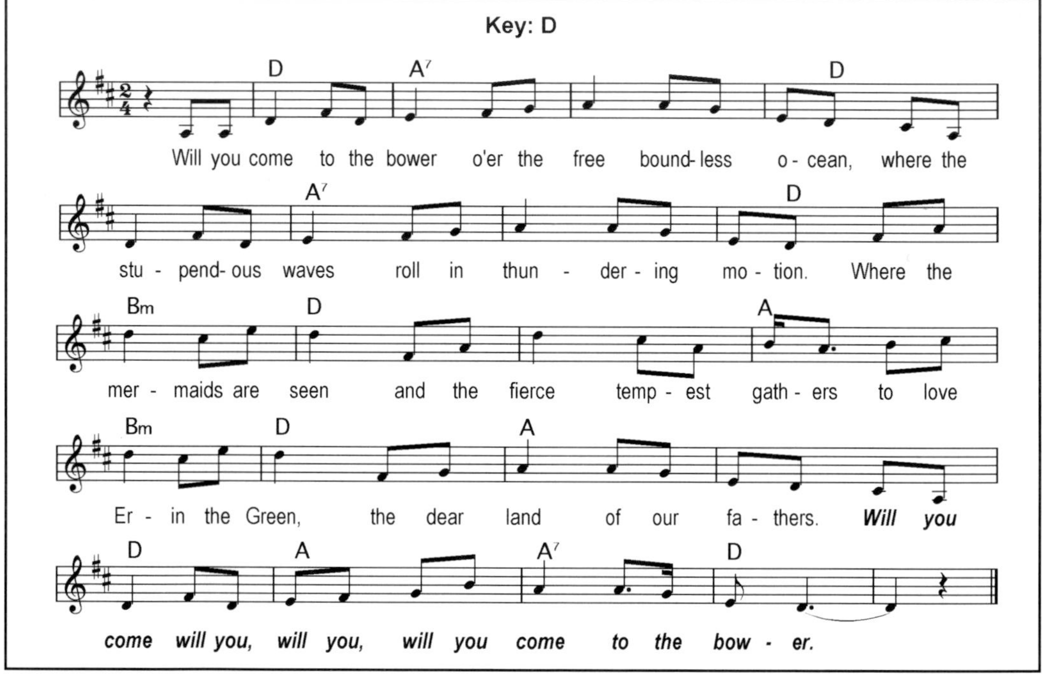

Will you come to the land of O'Neill and O'Donnell
Of Lord Lucan of old and immortal O'Connell
Where Brian drove the Danes and St. Patrick the vermin
And whose valleys remain still most beautiful and charming. ***Chorus***

You can visit Benburb and the storied Blackwater
Where Owen Roe met Munroe and his chieftains did slaughter
You may ride on the tide o'er the broad majestic Shannon
You may sail 'round Lough Neagh and see storied Dungannon. ***Chorus***

You can visit New Ross, gallant Wexford and Gorey
Where the green was last seen by proud Saxon and Tory
Where the soil is sanctified by the blood of each true man
Where they died, satisfied, their enemies they would not run from. ***Chorus***

Will you come and awake our lost land from its slumbers
And her fetters we will break; links that long are encumbered
And the air will resound with 'Hosannas' to greet you
On the shore will be found gallant Irishmen to meet you. ***Chorus***

St. Catherine's Church, Thomas Street, Dublin
Scene of Robert Emmet's execution on 20th September 1803

Banna Strand

Banna Strand is on the shores of County Kerry in the south-east of Ireland.

This song relates to a famous and fateful incident which took place during the lead-up to the Easter Rising of 1916 and involved the Irish patriot, Sir Roger Casement (1864 - 1916). Born in Sandycove, County Dublin into an Ulster Protestant family, Casement joined the British Colonial Service in 1892. He won international acclaim for his courageous reports on the exploitation of native workers by the rubber planters in the Belgian Congo and the Putamayo area of Peru. He received a knighthood for his achievements in 1911 and retired from the Colonial Services in 1913.

Casement was an Irish Nationalist at heart and was involved in the foundation of the Irish Volunteers. He firmly believed that an uprising against Britain could not be successful without German assistance.

In 1914 he travelled to Berlin to seek aid from the Germans for an uprising in Ireland against Britain. The German authorities agreed to send a shipload of arms and ammunition to Ireland and Casement set sail aboard the 'Aud', bound for Ireland, on April 9th, 1916.

When she arrived off the coast of Kerry the 'Aud' was to receive a signal from land and thus would commence the unloading of the valuable cargo. But no signal came. The arrangement was that two green fishing lamps would give the signal from land.

These lamps had been collected in Dublin three weeks earlier and were hanging in the Volunteer's drill-hall in Tralee.

The local Volunteer leaders had been told by Dublin that the 'Aud' would not arrive before the evening of Easter Sunday, April 23rd.

However the 'Aud' arrived on Holy Thursday and waited anxiously and in vain for a signal from shore. As the Irish coastline was being extensively patrolled by the British Navy it was only a matter of time before she would raise suspicions.

After a few close encounters during which the captain of the 'Aud', Lieutenant Karl Spindler, successfully bluffed his adversaries, the captain of a British Navy sloop, 'Bluebell', became suspicious of this strange vessel lurking about in Tralee Bay and ordered the 'Aud' to accompany her to Cobh to be searched. Knowing he could not out-run 'Bluebell' Spindler scuttled his ship outside Cobh Harbour. The 20,000 rifles, 1 million rounds of ammunition and 10 machine guns (part of the spoils of Hindenburg's victory over the Russians at Tannenberg) sank with her to the bottom of the sea.

The real blame for this calamity must be directed at the leaders of the Rising and the German Admiralty. Originally the leaders requested that the arms be delivered sometime between Holy Thursday and Easter Monday and the Germans agreed to this. However in early April the leaders became concerned that, if the arms were to arrive on Holy Thursday, the British authorities would probably know all about the operation well before the start of the Rising and the vital element of surprise would be lost. They decided to change the plans and requested that the arms should not arrive until sometime after Easter Sunday.

As the First World War was still raging at the time direct communications between the United Kingdom (which included Ireland) and Germany was impossible, so the message to alter the landing arrangements was carried by a nationalist sympathiser to John Devoy, head of Clan na Gael in New York. He would then relay it to Germany.

In the meantime, satisfied that the change of plans would be successfully relayed to the Germans, the leaders of the Rising informed the Tralee Volunteers that the arms would not arrive until sometime after Easter Sunday.

However, the emissary did not arrive in New York until April 14th, and the 'Aud' had departed for Ireland five days earlier. When Devoy contacted the German Admiralty with the altered plans he was informed that there was no radio on board the 'Aud' and therefore they couldn't change the landing arrangements. Although Devoy vehemently insisted that he sent an urgent message back to Dublin to this effect, there is no record of any such message and the leaders of the Rising continued to plan as if the arms landing schedule had been altered.

And the Tralee Volunteers still continued to make their own plans under the erroneous assumption that the arms would not arrive until after Easter Sunday.

While the 'Aud' was anxiously waiting for a signal from the shore Casement had landed at Banna Strand in a small boat from the accompanying German submarine 'U.19'. On Good Friday he was arrested by two suspicious Royal Irish Constabulary officers at a prehistoric site known locally as McKenna's Fort.

The failure to land the ammunition and the subsequent arrest of Casement inspired Eoin McNeill, the Commander-in-Chief of the Irish Volunteers, to immediately cancel the plans for the 1916 Rising. He was considerably successful in his endeavours as only a handful of Volunteers turned out for 'manoeuvres' on Easter Monday.

Roger Casement was convicted of treason and hanged in Pentonville Prison, London, in August 1916. His trial for treason attracted world-wide attention.

Following on extensive negotiations between the Irish and British Governments Casement's remains were returned to Ireland in 1965 where he was honoured with a State Funeral.

For further information about the 1916 Easter Rising see the Additional Notes.

The 'Lonely Banna Strand', Kerry

"No signal answers from the shore" Sir Roger sadly said
"No comrades here to meet me; alas they must be dead
But I must do my duty and today I mean to land"
So in a small boat rowed ashore on the lonely Banna Strand.

The R.I.C*. were hunting for Sir Roger high and low
They found him in McKenna's Fort; said they "You are our foe"
Said he "I'm Roger Casement, I come to my native land
And I mean to free my countrymen on the lonely Banna Strand"

They took Sir Roger prisoner and sailed to London Town
And in the Tower they locked him up; a traitor to the Crown
Said he "I am no traitor" but on trial he had to stand
For bringing German rifles to the lonely Banna Strand.

'Twas in an English prison that they led him to his death
"I'm dying for my country" he said with his last breath
They buried him in British soil far from his native land
And the wild waves sang his requiem on the lonely Banna Strand.

*Royal Irish Constabulary

Boulavogue

This fine ballad was written by Patrick Joseph McCall (1861 - 1919).

P.J. McCall was born in Dublin in 1861. His works, "Fenian Nights Entertainments", told the stories of the Irish heroes and carried on the work of "The Nation" (see Additional Notes) in educating the Irish people about their history and heritage. He died in Dublin in 1919.

This emotive ballad and another called "Kelly from Killane" (also written by McCall - page 60) were both written in 1898 to mark the centenary of the 1798 Rebellion.

"Boulavogue" is regarded by many (including myself) as the anthem of the 1798 Rebellion in Wexford. It sets out a brief history of the rebellion which took place in the Wexford area using the exploits of Father John Murphy (c. 1753 - 1798) of Boulavogue, County Wexford as its main theme.

Father Murphy was curate of Boulavogue and was one of the leaders of the 1798 Rebellion in the south-east, although he was not a member of the United Irishmen. The proper Ordnance Survey spelling of the village is 'Boleyvogue' and it is situated about eight miles north-east of Enniscorthy.

Father Murphy was born near Ferns in County Wexford. Originally he was against the idea of a rebellion and encouraged his parishioners to surrender any weapons in their possession. However, when his church was burned by the North Cork militia on May 26th, along with about twenty cottages belonging to local farming families, he rapidly altered his opinion.

Motivated by the reports of atrocities committed by Government forces and loyalists at Dunlavin and Carnew, Father Murphy agreed to lead the local insurgents into revolt.

On the evening of May 26th a patrol of Yeomen from the nearby town of Camolin was sent to a farmhouse near the village of The Harrow to search for arms. They were under the command of a local gentleman loyal to the Crown by the name of Lieutenant Bookey. This patrol found their way blocked outside the Harrow by Father Murphy's men. In the ensuing skirmish Bookey and his assistant were killed and the remaining Yeomen fled. Father Murphy then sent a party of his men to raid the house of Lord Mountnorris at Camolin where there was a large stockpile of arms. Mountnorris was not in residence at the time and the insurgents plundered the house without interruption.

As local Government forces quickly closed in on his men Father Murphy decided to make a stand on Oulart Hill. Although ill-armed against the North Cork militia under the command of Colonel Foote the insurgents achieved a decisive victory at Oulart Hill on May 27th. They then marched on and captured the undefended town of Ferns and on May 28th captured Enniscorthy. However their luck changed on June 9th when Father Murphy's forces suffered a serious defeat at the Battle of Arklow with the loss of about three hundred men.

The Crown forces gradually regained control and following the defeat of the insurgents on June 21st 1798 at the Battle of Vinegar Hill, near Enniscorthy town, Father Murphy was captured at Tullow, Co. Carlow and hanged.

"Tubberneering" and "Ballyellis" are places in Wexford where battles occurred during the Rising. "Enniscorthy", traversed by the River Slaney, is a large town in Wexford which was taken by the insurgents in May 1798 but was recaptured by the English forces at the decisive Battle of Vinegar Hill.

For further information on the 1798 Rebellion and Yeomanry see the Additional Notes.

1798 Memorial, The Harrow, Wexford
Scene of Father John Murphy's first encounter with the loyalists in the 1798 Insurrection, on May 26th 1798. Lieutenant Bookey and a Mr. John Donavan were killed and the remainder of the Camolin Yeomen fled.

He led us on 'gainst the coming soldiers and the cowardly yeomen we put to flight
'Twas at the Harrow the boys of Wexford showed Bookey's regiment how men could fight
Look out for hirelings King George of England; search every kingdom where breathes a slave
For Father Murphy of County Wexford sweeps o'er the land like a mighty wave.

We took Camolin and Enniscorthy and Wexford, storming, drove out our foes
'Twas at Slieve Coilte our pikes were reeking with crimson blood of the beaten Yoes
At Tubberneering and Ballyellis full many a Hessian lay in his gore
Ah, Father Murphy, had aid come over, the Green Flag floated from shore to shore

At Vinegar Hill o'er the pleasant Slaney our heroes vainly stood back to back
And the Yeos of Tullow took Father Murphy and burned his body upon the rack
God grant you glory brave Father Murphy and open heaven to all your men
The cause that called you may call tomorrow in another fight for the Green again

The Croppy Boy

This song was written by William McBurney, a native of County Down, under the pseudonym of 'Carroll Malone'. It was first published in 'The Nation' newspaper in 1845, without an air. The air and lyrics were first published together in "National Songs of Ireland" edited by M.J. Murphy in 1892.

The air is "Cailín Ó Cois tSiúre Mé" ("I Am The Girl From The River Suir Side"). This air can be traced back to 1584 under the phonetic "Calino Casturame" and is mentioned in Shakespeare's "Henry V'" (Act IV, Scene IV) when Pistol in his gibberish shouts "Callen o casture me!" to the French soldier.

The rebels who took part in the 1798 Rebellion were known as 'Croppies' on account of their short cropped hair cut in the style of the revolutionaries in France.

There are differing points of view as to whether or not this ballad is based on actual events. In W.J. Fitzpatrick's 'The Sham Squire' there is related an incident which is virtually identical to the story told in this ballad, though whether or not that is based on fact is also open to debate.

There is another popular ballad called "The Croppy Boy" which begins, 'It was early early in the Spring, when small birds tune and thrushes sing', and pre-dates the ballad in this book. In that particular ballad the Croppy Boy is betrayed by his own people.

A "yeoman" was a member of a part-time local force established in 1796. It was composed of men loyal to the English crown and comprised mainly Protestant landowners and merchants. The force gained a reputation for indiscriminate and undisciplined sectarian violence.

'Ross' (New Ross) and 'Gorey' are towns which saw scenes of fierce fighting during the 1798 Rebellion. Passage is a town in Waterford where the Croppy Boy in the ballad is said to be buried (interestingly, there isn't a graveyard in the town).

Geneva Barracks was located a few miles from Passage overlooking Waterford Harbour. Geneva Barracks was a settlement built by a group of Swiss dissenters who had settled there in 1783. They subsequently abandoned it and the English authorities used it as a detention centre following the 1798 Rebellion - hence the unusual name.

For further information about the 1798 Rebellion and Yeomanry see the Additional Notes.

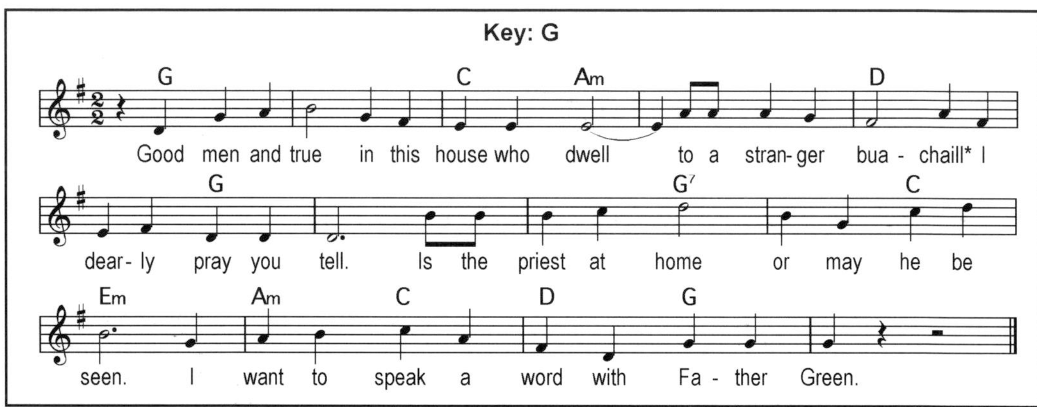

The youth has entered an empty hall, with lonely sounds does his light foot fall
And the gloomy chamber is cold and bare, with a vested priest in a lonely chair.

The youth has knelt to tell his sins; "Nomine Dei" the youth begins
At "mea culpa" he beats his breast; in broken murmurs he speaks the rest.

"At the siege of Ross did my father fall, and at Gorey my loving brothers all
I alone am left of my name and race; I will go to Wexford to take their place".

"I cursed three times since last Easter Day; at Mass-time once I went to play
I passed the churchyard one day in haste and forgot to pray for my mother's rest".

"I bear no hate against living things, but I love my country above my King
Now father bless me and let me go, to die if God has ordained it so".

The priest said naught, but a rustling noise made the youth look up in a wild surprise
The robes were off and in scarlet there sat a Yeoman captain with a fiery glare.

With fiery glare and with fury hoarse, instead of a blessing he breathed a curse
"'Twas a good thought, boy, to come here and shrive, for one short hour is your time to live".

"Upon yon river three tenders float; the priest is in one if he's not shot
We hold this house for our lord and King, and amen say I, may all traitors swing".

At Geneva Barracks that young man died and at Passage they have his body laid
Good people who live in peace and joy, now breath a prayer for the croppy boy.

*Pronounced "voukill" (boy)

1798 Memorial, New Ross, Wexford
The 1798 memorial in the form of a Croppy Boy situated in the centre of New Ross.

Joe Hill

This ballad is not of Irish origin but is a 'regular' at any Irish ballad session. It was written by the poet Alfred Hayes in 1925.

Joe Hill was born in Gavle, Sweden in 1879. His real name was Joel Emmanuel Haggland and he was one of a family of eight children whose father, Olof, was a railway worker. Life was tough in the Haggland family and deteriorated considerably when Olof died shortly after Joel's eighth birthday. In 1902 Joel decided to emigrate to America to make his fortune. Soon after his arrival in America with his brother Paul, Joel headed off to travel that vast land.

Sometime between 1906 and 1910 he changed his name to Joseph Hillstrom. In 1910 he joined a militant labour movement called the 'Industrial Workers of the World' and at that time changed his name to Joe Hill. During subsequent years he was an ardent labour activist in the front lines of many workers demonstrations.

Hill had a keen love of music and was self-taught on the piano, guitar and violin. He wrote many songs aimed at firing up the poorest of America's workers and several of these songs became 'labour anthems' during the militant labour demonstrations at the time.

Throughout this period of worker unrest Hill was under close observation by the authorities.

Hill arrived in Salt Lake City, Utah in the summer of 1913. On the night of January 10th 1914 there was an attempted robbery at a small grocery store and the two raiders shot dead the owner of the store, John Morrison and his son, Arling. During the gun battle it appeared that one of the raiders had also been shot.

At 11.00pm on the same night Joe Hill called to Doctor Frank McHugh with a bulletwound in his chest. He told the doctor that he had been shot during a row over a woman. While in the doctor's surgery a gun dropped from Hill's clothing. McHugh later said that he didn't get a good look at the gun as it was in its holster. After treatment a friend of the doctor's drove Hill home. On the journey Hill asked the driver to stop the car and Hill then apparently threw a gun into a nearby field.

When Doctor McHugh read of the raid on the Morrison grocery he contacted the police and Joe Hill was arrested. Pleading poverty Hill acted as his own lawyer during the preliminary hearing. During the trial itself (at which Hill was represented by two young Salt Lake City lawyers) it was assumed that Hill would testify in his own defence and explain the circumstances surrounding his gunshot wound and perhaps identify the 'woman' he had mentioned to Doctor McHugh. However, Hill refused to testify and speculation continues to this day as to why he made this decision. Acrimony also arose between Hill and his lawyers

On dubious identification evidence Hill was found guilty of murder and was sentenced to death.

Almost immediately his case became a 'cause celebre' for the Industrial Workers of the World who claimed that Hill's conviction was orchestrated by 'Big Business'. Workers' rallies were held throughout America and Hill himself claimed that he had been denied a fair trial. In one of his last messages from his death row cell Joe Hill sent a telegram to his comrade "Big Bill" Haywood. The message would emerge as a rallying cry for downtrodden workers for many years - "Don't waste time mourning. Organise!"

Joe Hill was executed by firing squad on the morning of November 19th, 1915.

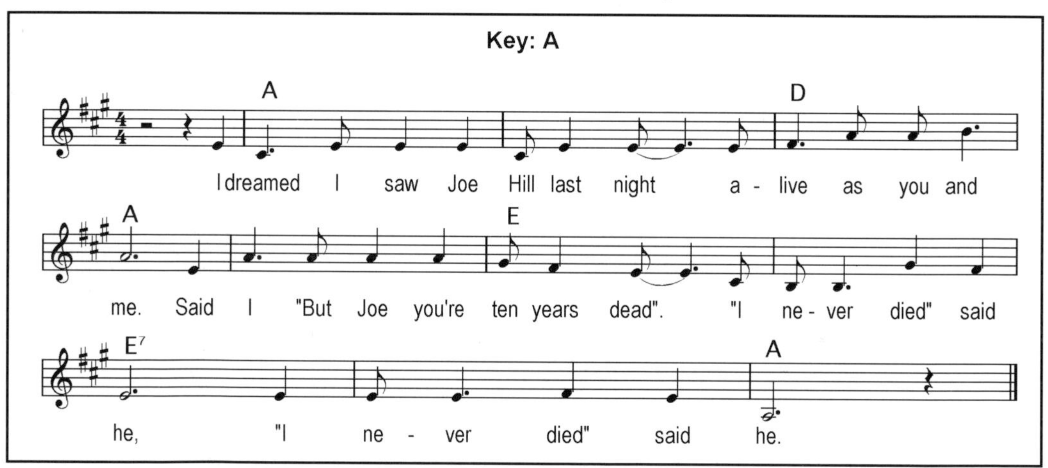

"In Salt Lake City, Joe", said I, him standing by my side
"They framed you on a murder charge". Said Joe "I never died"
Said Joe "I never died".

"The copper bosses shot you, Joe; they filled you full of lead"
"Takes more than guns to kill a man" said Joe, "and I ain't dead"
Said Joe "and I ain't dead".

And there he stood as large as life and smiling with his eyes
Said Joe "what they forgot to kill went on to organise
Went on the organise".

From San Diego up to Maine in every mine and mill
Where working men defend their rights it's there you'll find Joe Hill
It's there you'll find Joe Hill.

(Repeat first verse)

Kilmainham Gaol, Dublin
The main gate through which many insurgents and nationalists passed during the life of the prison

The West's Awake

This ballad was written by Thomas Davis (1814 - 1845) to the old Irish air "The Brink of the White Rock". Davis was born in Mallow, Co. Cork. The son of an English army surgeon and Irish Protestant mother he was educated at Trinity College Dublin. The ballad, along with many others written by Davis, reflects the aspiration of the Young Ireland movement of the 1840's of which he was leader.

Davis espoused many of his thoughts and ideas for Irish Nationhood in 'The Nation', a weekly newspaper which he founded in October 1842. He also sought to awaken a sense of Irish nationalistic sentiment and pride among Irish people through the many ballads published in 'The Nation', this being one of them. He also wrote another ballad in this book, "A Nation Once Again" (page 62).

Davis died suddenly in September 1845 from an attack of scarlet fever at the age of 31 years.

For further information on Young Ireland and 'The Nation' see the Additional Notes.

That chainless wave and lovely land; Freedom and Nationhood demand
Be sure the great God never planned; for trodden slaves a home so grand
For long a proud and haughty race; honoured and sentinelled the place
Sing, Oh! Not e'en their sons' disgrace; can quite destroy their glory's trace.

For often in O'Connor's van; to triumph dashed each Connaught clan
As fleet as deer the Normans ran; through Curlew's Pass and Ardrahan
And later times saw deeds so brave; and glory guards Clanricard's grave
Sing, Oh! They died their land to save; at Aughrim's plains and Shannon's wave.

And if when all a vigil keep; the West's asleep, the West's asleep
Alas as well may Erin weep; that Connaught lies in slumber deep
But hark, a voice like thunder spake; the West's awake, the West's awake
Sing, Oh! Hurrah, let England quake; we'll watch till death for Erin's sake.

(Verse and chorus have the same melody)

This ballad was originally known as "The Last Moments Of Robert Emmet". The song first appeared on broadsides around 1900. The text is sometimes ascribed to Tom Maguire, member of the Irish Republican Brotherhood, Commander of the Fermanagh Brigade of the IRA and member of the first Irish Parliament (Dail).

This ballad mourns the plight of one of Ireland's most popular, and least successful, insurgents, Robert Emmet (1778 - 1803). Emmet was one of a new group of nationalist activists to emerge following the defeat of the 1798 Rebellion. For further information on Robert Emmet see the Additional Notes.

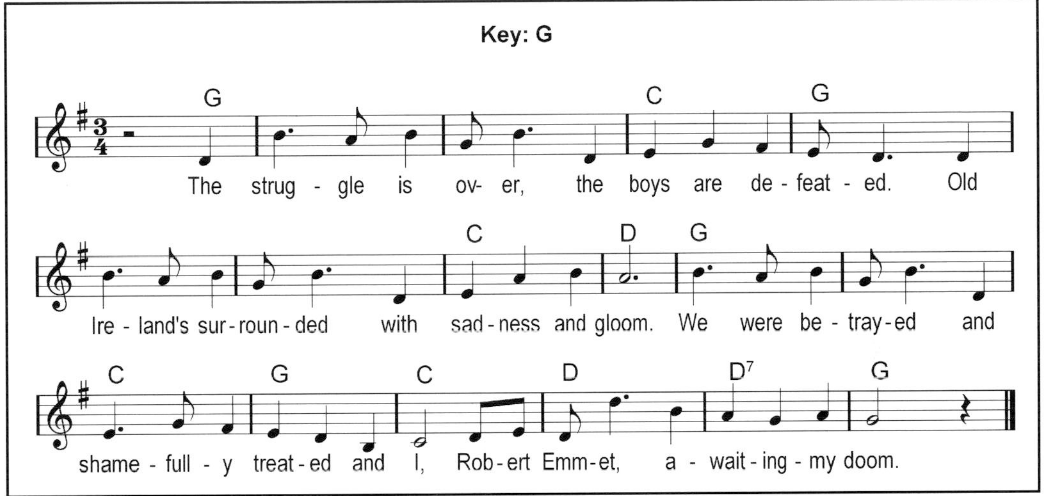

Bold Robert Emmet, The darling of Erin
Bold Robert Emmet will die with a smile
Farewell companions, both loyal and daring
I'll lay down my life for the Emerald Isle

Hung drawn and quartered, sure that was my sentence; But soon I will show them no coward am I
My crime was the love of the land I was born in; a hero I lived and a hero I'll die. ***Chorus***

The barque lay at anchor awaiting to bring me; over the billows to the land of the free
But I must see my sweetheart, I know she will cheer me; and with her I will sail over the sea

But I was arrested and cast into prison; tried as a traitor, a rebel, a spy
But no one dare call me a knave or a coward; a hero I lived and a hero I'll die. ***Chorus***

Hark, the bell's tolling, I well know it's meaning; my poor heart tells me it is my death knell
In come the clergy, the warder is leading; I have no friends here to bid me farewell

Goodbye old Ireland, my parents and sweetheart; companions in arms to forget you must try
I am proud of the honour, it was only my duty; a hero I lived and a hero I'll die. ***Chorus***

"Let no man write my epitaph; for as no man who knows my motives dares now vindicate them, let not prejudice or ignorance asperse them. Let them rest in obscurity and peace; my memory be left in oblivion and my tomb remain uninscribed, until other times and other men can do justice to my character. When my country takes its place among the nations of this earth, then, and not till then, let my epitaph be written. I have done"
The conclusion of Robert Emmet's famous 'Speech from the Dock', 19 September 1803

Arthur McBride

This old anti-recruitment ballad was probably written during the Napoleonic Wars (1792 - 1815), hence the reference to France. It is believed that the song originated in Ireland but versions of it are also known in England and Scotland. The song was collected by W.P. Joyce in the 1840's and around the same time the ballad collector George Petrie received a version from Donegal.

It was the practice of Recruiting Sergeants in the British Army to tempt young, impressionable and destitute men to enlist by offering them the immediate payment of a shilling. They were also bombarded with romantic descriptions of a soldier's life. Many succumbed to the temptation, much to their later regret. The practice was known as 'taking the King's shilling' and was discontinued in 1879.

The Recruiting Sergeant was one of the most hated persons in Ireland. For many of the destitute Irish peasants the only hope of escaping starvation was to join the British army and thus fight for a power which they despised. Foot soldiers were subjected to terrible conditions in the British Army and discipline was strict and harsh. The minimum punishment for misdemeanours was 25 lashes of the cat-o'-nine-tails and the maximum was 1500 lashes! Anti-recruitment ballads became very popular throughout the 19th and early 20th centuries with such songs as "Johnny I Hardly Knew Ye" (page 32), "Mrs. McGrath" (page 34) and "The Kerry Recruit" (page 38).

I have come across two fine, and very different, versions of this ballad recorded by Irish artists. One was recorded by the folk group Planxty on an album called "Planxty" - very similar to this version. The other version was recorded by Paul Brady on the album "Andy Irvine & Paul Brady". Both recordings were made in the 1970's and are available today on CD.

He said "My young fellows if you will enlist; a guinea you quickly will have in your fist
And besides a whole crown for to kick up the dust; and drink the King's health till the morning"
Had we been such fools as to take the advance; with the wee bit of money we'd have to run chance
"For you'd think it no scruples to send us to France; where we would be killed in the morning".

He said "My young fellows if I hear but one word; I instantly now will out with my sword
And into your bodies as strength will afford; so now my gay devils take warning"
But Arthur and I we soon took the odds; and gave them no time for to draw out their blades
Our trusty shillelaghs came over their heads; and paid them right smart in the morning.

As for the wee drummer we rifled his pouch; and we made a football of his rowdy-dow-dow
And into the ocean to rock and to roll; and bade him a tedious returning
As for the old rapier that hung by his side; we flung it as far as we could in the tide
"To the devil I pitch you" said Arthur McBride; "to temper your steel in the morning".

This ballad was written by Anna Johnston (1866 - 1902) under the pseudonym 'Ethna Carbury'. She was born in Ballymena in County Antrim. She was the editor of the Belfast Republican journal "The Sean Van Vocht" ("The Poor Old Woman") with Alice Milligan.
She married the folklorist and storyteller Seamus McManus from Mountcharles in County Donegal in 1902. Her poetry and that of her husband was published in a volume called "We Sang for Ireland" (1902).
This ballad has the same air as "Sean South from Garryowen" (page 56) and is dedicated to the memory of Roddy McCorley, a patriot who took part in the 1798 Rebellion in County Antrim. McCorley was a Presbyterian from Duneane. He was on the run for over a year after the rebellion but was betrayed and was hanged in the town of Toome Bridge in County Antrim (Northern Ireland) on February 28th, 1800. It is said that his body was buried directly beneath the gallows.
Ironically, Toome Bridge derives its name from the Irish word 'Tuaim' meaning 'burial mound'.
For further information about the 1798 Rebellion see the Additional Notes.

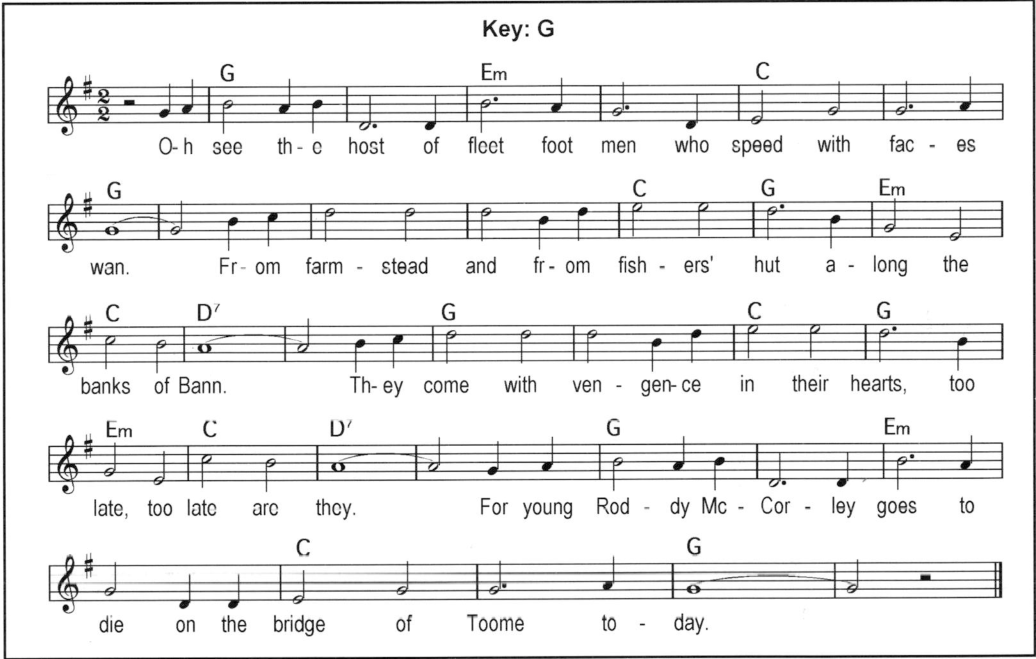

When he last stepped up that street, his shining pike in hand
Behind him marched in grim array a stalwart earnest band
For Antrim town, for Antrim town he led them to the fray
And young Roddy McCorley goes to die on the bridge of Toome today.

Up the narrow streets he boldly steps, smiling, proud and young
Around the hemp rope on his neck his golden ringlets clung
There was never a tear in his blue eyes, both sad and bright are they
For young Roddy McCorley goes to die on the bridge of Toome today

There was never a one of all our dead more bravely fell in fray
Than he who marches to his fate on the bridge of Toome today
True to the last as we say goodbye he treads the upward way
And young Roddy McCorley goes to die on the bridge of Toome today.

"I have reason to think more men than fell in battle were slain in cold blood. No quarter was given to persons taken prisoner as rebels with or without arms..... How many people fell in this manner, or were put to death unresisting in houses, fields and elsewhere, would be as difficult to state with accuracy as the number slain in battle"
Contemporaneous account of the aftermath of the 1798 Rebellion in Wexford by the loyalist James Gandon, in his book, 'History of the Rebellion in Ireland in 1798' (Dublin 1801)

The Bard Of Armagh

This ballad is also known as "Brady's Lament".
The County of Armagh is situated in the north-east of Ireland. It is the smallest of the six counties of Northern Ireland. County Wexford is situated in the south-east of Ireland. I can't find any "Durrish" in Ireland but there is a small village in County Cork called Durrus so this may be the place referred to by Bold Phelim Brady.
The air of this ballad was also used in the popular American country song "The Streets of Laredo".

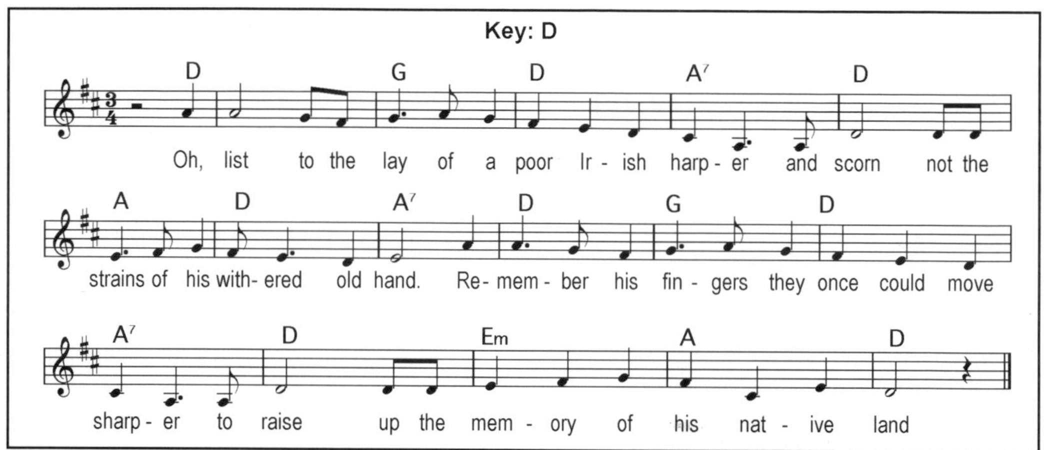

When I was a young lad King Jamie did flourish
And I followed the wars with my brogues bound with straw
And all the fair colleens from Wexford to Durrish
Called me Bold Phelim Brady, the Bard of Armagh.

How I love for to muse on the days of my boyhood
Though four score and three years have flitted since then
Still it gives sweet reflections as every young joy should
For light-hearted boys make the best of old men.

At pattern or fair I could twist my shillelagh
Or trip through a jig with me brogues bound with straw
Whilst all the pretty maidens around me assembled
For Bold Phelim Brady, the Bard of Armagh.

Although I have travelled this wide world all over
But Erin's my home and a parent to me
Then oh, let the ground that my old bones will cover
Be cut from the soil that is trod by the free.

And when Sergeant Death in his arms shall embrace me
Oh lull me to sleep with sweet 'Erin go Brath'*
By the side of my young wife, dear Kathleen, oh place me
Then forget Phelim Brady, the Bard of Armagh.

*Pronounced "Erin go bra" (Ireland forever!)

MEMORIAL TO MICHAEL COLLINS AT BÉAL NA BLATH, CORK
Collins, political and military leader of Republicans during the War of Independence, was shot dead here in an ambush at the closing stages of the Irish Civil War, on 22nd August 1922

Sam Hall

This old ballad also goes under the title of "Jack Hall" and probably relates to a chimney sweep named Jack Hall who was a well-known burglar. He was hanged for his crimes in 1701. In the 1850's a music hall entertainer, C.W. Ross, gained quite a reputation for singing a bawdy version of this ballad. There is another English ballad with the same rhythm and word pattern called "Captain Kidd" who ironically was hanged for piracy in London in the same year as Jack Hall.

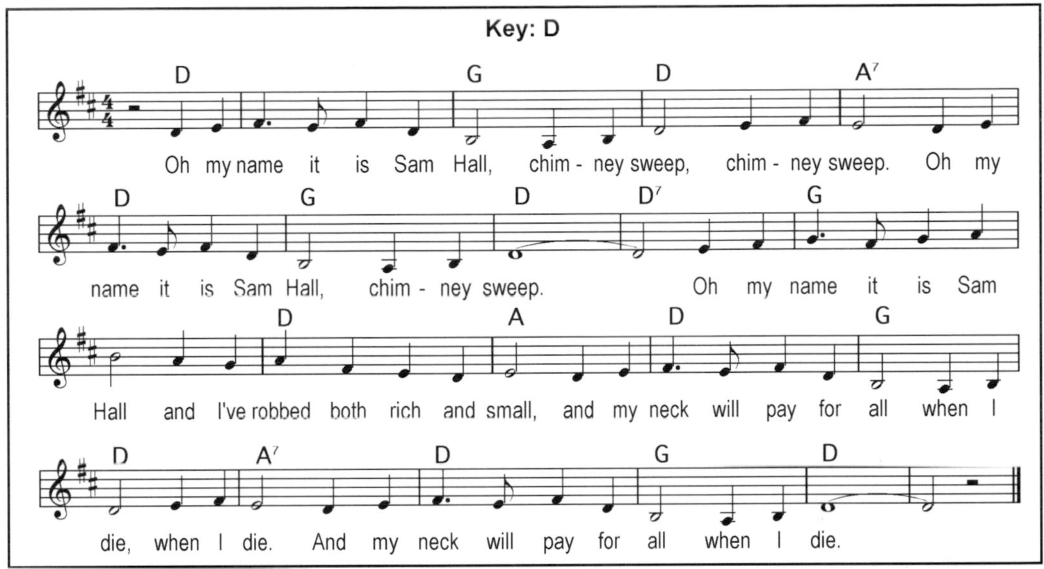

Oh they took me to Coote Hill in a cart, in a cart
Oh they took me to Coote Hill in a cart
Oh they took me to Coote Hill and 'twas there I made my will
For the best of friends must part; so must I, so must I
For the best of friends must part; so must I.

Now the preacher he did come, he did come, he did come
Of the preacher he did come, he did come
Oh the preacher he did come and he looked so doggone glum
And he talked of Kingdom Come with a tear, with a tear
And he talked of Kingdom Come with a tear.

Up the ladder I did grope; that's no joke, that's no joke
Up the ladder I did grope; that's no joke
Up the ladder I did grope and the hangman pulled the rope
And ne'er a word I spoke; tumbling down, tumbling down
And ne'er a word I spoke; tumbling down.

(Repeat first verse)

Kilmainham Gaol, Dublin
The door to Padraig Pearse's cell, through which he was led to his execution on May 3rd, 1916

The Rocks Of Bawn

In this ballad the singer tells of the wretched plight of the farm labourer, and he wishes that the Recruiting Sergeant would recruit him into the army so that he would escape the misery of working for a miserly farmer. In the first verse he warns all potential labourers to be very careful when they are making their bargains at the hiring fair.
The hiring of farm labour through the hiring fairs was very common during the late 19th century. At these fairs farmers and those seeking work would negotiate wages and conditions of work. They were most popular in Ulster (Northern Ireland) and were usually held twice a year - in May and November. Working contracts were for a six month period.
The largest fairs were held in the Ulster towns of Derry, Strabane, Letterkenny and Omagh.
The hiring fairs began to disappear at the beginning of the 20th century and for a while many of them evolved into social occasions and local festivals.

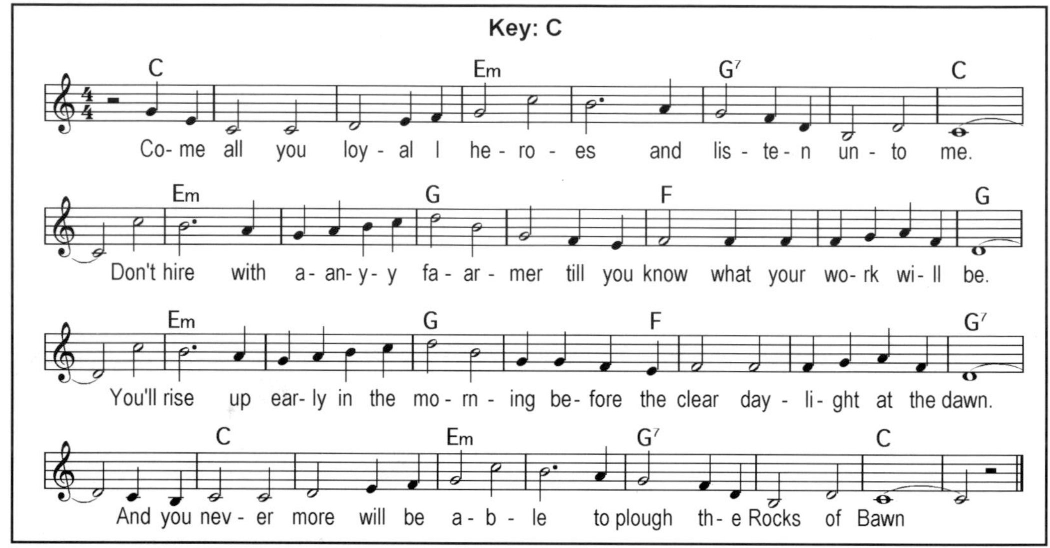

My shoes they are all worn and my stockings they are thin
My heart is always trembling now for fear they might give in
My heart is always trembling now from the clear daylight till the dawn
And I never will be able to plough the Rocks of Bawn.

My curse upon you Sweeney boy, you have me nearly robbed
You're sitting by the fireside now, your feet upon the hob
You're sitting by the fireside now from the clear daylight till the dawn
And you never will be able to plough the Rocks of Bawn

Rise up gallant Sweeney, and get your horses hay
And give them a good feed of oats before they start away
Don't feed them on soft turnip sprigs that grow on yon green lawn
Or they never will be able to plough the Rocks of Bawn.

I wish the Sergeant-Major would send for me in time
And place me in some regiment while in my youth and prime
I'd fight for Ireland's glory now from the clear daylight till the dawn
Before I would return again to plough the Rocks of Bawn.

Garden Of Remembrance, Parnell Square, Dublin.
The Garden, opened in 1966, is a memorial to those who gave their lives throughout the course of Irish history in the struggle for Irish independence

Removal of CD

Carefully remove the CD from the CD sleeve.

Your CD can be stored in this CD sleeve, which is permanently fixed to the book cover so that you can keep it safely with the book at all times.

Do not attempt to remove the CD sleeve from the cover of the book as it will result in damage to the book